Scottish Education Department

**Scottish Central Committee on English**

# Scottish Literature in the Secondary School

A report of a Sub-committee
on the study of
Scottish Literature in Schools

Edinburgh   Her Majesty's Stationery Office

ISBN 0 11 491371 4

'For I marvell gretlie, I yow assure,
Considderand the peple and the ground,
That Ryches suld nocht in this realme redound.'

Sir David Lindsay: 'Of the Realme of Scotland'

# Contents

Additional items exemplifying the use of Scots material for early stage pupils and for older non-academic pupils are available from the Director, Centre for Information on the Teaching of English, Moray House College of Education, Holyrood Road, Edinburgh, EH8 8AQ.

# Membership of the Sub-Committee

Miss M. D. W. Keaney, Craiglockhart College of Education, Edinburgh (Chairman)
Mr J. N. Alison, Hazlehead Academy, Aberdeen (from 1st May, 1973)
Mr J. D. Blackburn, Moray House College of Education, Edinburgh (formerly Golspie High School)
Miss J. Bowie, St. Margaret's School, Edinburgh
Mr J. B. Caird, H.M. Inspector of Schools (until September, 1974)
Mr G. W. Coe, Preston Lodge High School, Prestonpans
Mr B. D. J. Denoon, Inverness High School
Mr T. D. Gifford, University of Strathclyde, Glasgow (until July, 1973)
Mr A. Johnstone, Adviser in English, Tayside Region.
Dr J. T. Low, Moray House College of Education, Edinburgh (until July, 1974)
Mr Robert Millar, Director, C.I.T.E. (until September, 1973)
Mr G. Waddell, Gatehouse Secondary School, Gatehouse of Fleet
Mr D. Chalmers, Penicuik High School (Secretary)

Also associated: Mr S. B. Smyth, Director, C.I.T.E.

The Sub-committee wishes to acknowledge the help given by Mr Tom Allan of Boroughmuir Secondary School, Edinburgh in the compilation of the list of Children's Fiction with a Scottish Setting; by Dr W. R. Aitken of Strathclyde University in the checking of bibliographical details; by Mrs Gillian Blackmore, Librarian, C.I.T.E., for work on the booklists; and by Miss Aileen Mitchell, Secretary, C.I.T.E., in the typing (and frequent re-typing) of the manuscript of this document.

# Preface

In 1972, the newly-formed Scottish Central Committee on English appointed a sub-committee to investigate the place of Scottish literature in an English curriculum. In so doing they were fulfilling the intentions of the former Central Committee on English which had planned the production of a report on this topic.

The terms of the remit given to the sub-committee were: to discuss the place of Scottish literature in an English curriculum, to select a corpus of literature for use in secondary schools and to suggest aims and methods of presentation for the different stages of the secondary school.

The definition of the term Scottish literature was the sub-committee's first concern. For the purposes of this document Scottish literature is defined in the following terms: writings about the experience of people living in Scotland, and works which are concerned with experiences furth of Scotland of any writer who is a Scot or who has lived long enough in Scotland to be regarded as a Scot. It follows therefore that Scottish literature embraces writings in Scots, English and Gaelic in translation. One of the first decisions of the sub-committee was that it was competent to deal with Gaelic literature only in translation.

A document dealing with Scottish literature must inevitably make recommendations of a literary nature: it must refer to the wealth of material available in poetry; it must indicate the offerings of the less rich area of prose; and it must catalogue the rather meagre crop of drama. However, there is also in this document a conscious attempt to interpret literature generously by including documentary, photographic and musical material and by giving due consideration to the world of fiction for the adolescent.

In our suggestions we have tried, as far as possible, to draw on works which are currently in print and reasonably accessible; but it is a sad fact that much valuable material is out of print and that even relatively recent works fall out of print quickly and are not re-issued. We make no apology for recommending out of print texts: it is only as a result of demand that these come to be reprinted, and one of our concerns is to stimulate such a demand.

We concern ourselves with aims, materials and methods of presentation for the following stages of the secondary school: the early stages, the older non-academic pupils, fourth and fifth year certificate pupils, and post-Higher pupils. The needs of middle stage certificate pupils are not dealt with separately, but suitable texts and approaches can be selected from the chapters on the early stages and on fourth and fifth year pupils.

Finally, we invited two acknowledged authorities to make statements on important areas that did not quite fall within our remit but which, we felt, could not be ignored: Gaelic literature, and the Scots language.

# Acknowledgements

We are grateful to the following for permission to reproduce copyright material:

J. M. Dent & Sons Ltd. for extracts from *Highland Year* by Lea MacNally;
Penguin Books Ltd. for extracts from *Ring of Bright Water* by Gavin Maxwell;
Charles Lavell Ltd. for an extract from *The Singing Forest* by H. Mortimer Batten;
Oxford University Press for extracts from *Scottish Folk Tales and Legends* by Barbara Ker-Wilson;
David Higham Associates Ltd. for the short story *The Kitten* by Alexander Reid;
Lutterworth Press for an extract from *String Lug the Fox* by David Stephen.

We have also made use of material from Joseph Jacobs's *Celtic Fairy Tales* (The Bodley Head) and Norman Buchan's *101 Scottish Songs* (Collins) both of which are out of copyright.

**The Report**

# The Place of Scottish Literature in an English Curriculum

'There comes a time when out of respect for itself a country must collect its resources and look at its assets and shortcomings with an eye that is both sharp and warm; see what is there, what is not there, what could be there.'
Edwin Morgan: 'The Resources of Scotland'
*Times Literary Supplement*, 28th July, 1972.

One of the ways in which any society attempts to lead its young to an understanding of what they are as individual and social beings is by introducing to them the literature of their own country, from its nursery and folk tales to the achievements of its best writers past and present. French children study French literature, German children study German literature, English children study English literature.

In Scotland, things have been different. Scottish children read, in the main, English literature; the place given in the past to Scottish literature has been peripheral and continues to be so in the present. Why this should be defies easy generalisation, but part of the explanation is to be found within the educational system itself, viewed over the past hundred years of compulsory schooling.

What we find is not total neglect. National examinations recognised certain Scottish classics—ballads, the poems of Burns, novels by Scott and Stevenson. The Advisory Council's report on *Primary Education* (1946) accorded, in Chapter XII (pp. 71–81), a place to Scottish culture in education*, even if it did present an inadequate account of Scottish literature and a limited appreciation of the qualities of the vernacular.

Valuable contributions were made by individuals such as Sir William Craigie, a noted protagonist for Scots in schools, and by organisations such as the Burns Federation and the Saltire Society. The Educational Institute of Scotland published in the *Scottish Educational Journal* in 1925 Hugh MacDiarmid's influential essays, later collected under the title of *Contemporary Scottish Studies*. The Lanarkshire local association of the E.I.S. did pioneering work in producing the *Lanimer Books of Verse*, while the Glasgow local association produced, in 1933–34, a report on the educational significance of Glasgow speech.

Although the range of texts produced for use in schools was limited, some were available e.g. *Barbour's Bruce—Selections for use in Schools* (1909), *Readings in Modern Scots* (1913), *The Northern Muse* (1924), *Oor Mither Tongue* (1937), and *A Scots Reader*

*Reprinted as an appendix in *Secondary Education* (1947).

(1937–39). This is not a complete list, but the range was limited and the cover patchy.

Official and semi-official policy has never explicitly discouraged the inclusion in educational practice of an element of Scottish language, literature and culture. Where positive encouragement was given, however, it was, in the main, too generalised or fragmentary to off-set the other influences inhibiting a confident and balanced approach to the teaching of Scottish literature in Scottish schools.

Scottish teachers themselves have been inadequately prepared to teach Scottish literature. Until very recently there was no chair of Scottish Literature in any Scottish university. Most of those who were to become teachers of English in our schools were trained to value English literature, and—by neglect, in the main, rather than by intent—to undervalue Scots. The critical insights and scholarly apparatus by which students come to recognise the significance and worth of works of literature were brought to bear, at best, on only a very restricted range of Scottish texts and writers, and then sometimes from the perspective of the English literary tradition: the Makars were 'Scottish Chaucerians'; Burns was a pre-Romantic.

Teachers, of course, do not spring fully armed from their universities and colleges. They continue their education informally both from the established practices of the schools in which they teach, and from those sources in the general culture that are available to all. Neither conduced to giving Scottish literature the attention it deserved. In schools, the great determinant of syllabi was the literature paper of English at Higher Grade. In spite of the invariable presence in the examination of the chance to write about Scottish literature, most teachers, in the interest of their pupils' examination success, chose for study lists of texts almost exclusively English. Although these lists included, quite rightly, the masterpieces of English literature, they included, with less justification, some quite minor works as well. Such a tradition, once established, is not easily broken.

Outwith the classroom, books, newspapers, cinema, radio and, later, television, operated on teachers and pupils alike in favour of English and mid-Atlantic culture, and their influence was inevitably reflected in the day-to-day work in Scottish schools.

There were teachers who, in the face of these influences, helped their pupils to develop an interest in a range of Scottish works, but these teachers were to a large degree self-taught. In recent years, however, there have been signs of changing attitudes and of an increased awareness of the need for concerted action.

Of first importance in the creation of this change have been, appropriately enough, Scottish writers themselves. Such has been the flowering of literature in this century that it would have been impossible to ignore. This literary revival began at the turn of the century, but the obvious development has been from the twenties onward.

In prose, the novels of Grassic Gibbon and of Neil Gunn are probably the main achievements, but there has been much else. And the output continues. Over the last few years, new writers, particularly from the industrial areas in the West of Scotland, have been making their presence felt. In drama there have been surges of activity. Tyrone Guthrie's revival in 1948 of *The Thrie Estaits* was the prime mover in a minor renaissance in drama in which Kemp, McLellan and Reid helped to develop both Scottish Community Drama and professional theatre. The plays of Bridie were a major contribution and recently there have been some vigorous plays emanating from the Glasgow area and gaining ready audiences.

It is, however, with the poets that the main impetus has been. The part played by MacDiarmid in campaigning, both in poetry and elsewhere, for Scots literature and language scarcely needs to be recounted. Suffice it to record that he and the other notable poets who have flourished since the twenties have produced a first-rate corpus of poetry both in Scots and in English. And, for those who have access to it, there is the poetry in Gaelic of Sorley MacLean, Iain Crichton Smith and others. Poetry, indeed, is probably more alive in Scotland at present than it has been at any time before—witness the popularity of poetry circles, festivals and conferences and the number and variety of poets, established and lesser-known, whose work appears in current periodicals like *Lines Review* and *Akros*.

Encouraging this vitality is the Scottish Arts Council with its awards to writers, its support of the Writers in Schools project and its recently introduced scheme for Writers in Residence in major Scottish cities.

In academic circles, the status of Scottish literature is higher now than it has ever been: in almost all the Scottish universities it is now possible to take courses in Scottish literature; a Department of Scottish Literature exists in Glasgow University; and in Edinburgh, there is a Chair of Scottish Literature and Oral Traditions and the well-established School of Scottish Studies. *The Scottish National Dictionary* (*ed.* D. Murison) and *The Dictionary of the Older Scottish Tongue* (*ed.* A. J. Aitken) have provided a reliable scholarly base for literary studies as well as a word hoard for creative writers. The Association for Scottish Literary Studies, representative of creative writers, academics and critics, has sponsored the publication and re-issue of important works and promotes the study, teaching and writing of Scottish literature. The universities have also encouraged contemporary writing by appointing Writers in Residence and founding Fellowships in Creative Writing; and the Universities Committee on Scottish Literature has been another academic agency for promoting interest in Scottish literature.

The active involvement of practising teachers in fostering Scottish literature studies is reflected in the production of stimulating classroom material by Local Development Committees from Shetland in the north to Wigtownshire in the south-west. *Teaching English*, the C.I.T.E. journal, also publishes articles and reviews on Scottish topics. In Edinburgh, the Committee for the Advancement of Scottish Literature in Schools, originally an L.D.C., has worked in conjunction with local authorities, advisers and colleges of education in organising conferences and in-service courses.

Assistance has also been given by the Scottish Arts Council, The Saltire Society, the Schools Broadcasting Council for Scotland and the B.B.C. *Scottish Writing Today*, a radio programme for fifth and sixth years, both met a demand and stimulated interest. A Scottish magazine programme for younger pupils began in the autumn of 1974. Publishers, too, have recognised the demand for Scottish literature and have made some efforts to satisfy it, but we would emphasise that much still remains to be done in this area.

Despite this very positive current of interest the future of Scottish literature teaching in schools is in delicate balance. The Scottish literary tradition is a strong one, certainly in poetry. But no tradition, however strong, can survive neglect. The continuation and strengthening of this tradition is—partly but importantly—in the hands of Scottish teachers and to this end it behoves them to evaluate the considerable corpus of Scottish literature and to decide what and how much to introduce to their pupils.

In doing this, they will bring to bear educational criteria and values; they will seek to serve the needs and interests of the boys and girls they teach. We are convinced that teachers, with these criteria in mind, will find a substantial body of texts suitable for all ages and stages in the secondary school.

They will find texts that have a special relevance to the lives of their pupils. The images that Scottish writers create are drawn from the world which pupils know; the attitudes they deal with, the moral stances they take, reflect aspects of the pupils' own world; the language (or languages) they are written in reflects, in the way that literary languages in any culture do, the varieties of language that they hear spoken and that they speak themselves.

These varieties include Scots dialect material. We have no hesitation in advocating its use. The stress placed by contemporary linguistic science on 'variety' and 'appropriateness' encourages us in the view that Scots and Standard English (so-called) are mutually enriching, and that acquaintance with texts in dialect is likely to extend language competence rather than, as was at one time supposed, to stultify it. For similar reasons we advocate the study of texts written in English by native speakers of Gaelic and of translations from Gaelic. Both sorts of texts are likely to employ linguistic structures that reflect the features of the native language and thus, potentially, enlarge the students' awareness of language.

So far we argue for the increased consideration of Scots literature on grounds both familiar and, we believe, acceptable to English teachers: that it contains works that serve the developmental needs of the pupils; that it is relevant to the life that they live; that sections of it will contribute in a special way to their language competence.

There is another consideration. It is fashionable to talk of schools and teachers serving the needs and interests of their pupils. Less common is the recognition that those needs and interests are inevitably formulated by the teacher, who has to be alert not only to the children with whom he works, but also to the changing world of which he and they are a part, and into full membership of which they are moving. A feature of this world is its tendency to develop larger and larger administrative units in government and business and for popular entertainment to become more and more homogenised and pre-packaged. As this tendency grows, so does the need for the individual to discover and define himself in terms of the local and national (as opposed to the international or supra-national) culture.

In presenting these considerations, we are not, of course, advocating the wholesale abandonment of the study of English (and other) texts in favour of Scottish ones. Scottish children belong to a particular local area; they belong to Scotland; they are citizens of the United Kingdom; they are part of the world-wide community of nations whose first language is English; and the tradition of Western European civilisation is their tradition as well. What we argue is that there should be in schools balanced programmes of literary studies which reflect all these cultural influences. This would mean that in many schools Scottish literature would have to be given a more significant place than it has had in the past.

In general, we hold that Scottish texts present essentially the same teaching problems as any other literary material. However, there are four distinct challenges facing the teacher who wishes to use Scottish texts and we set them forth here because they have a bearing on all the recommendations that we make for every stage. Scottish writers of every century, including our own, show a preoccupation with the national past; the bulk of Scottish literature is concerned with the rural rather than the urban scene; much of the material is strongly localised and some localities are much richer in materials than others; and the Scots language in its variations of dialects and orthographies is often an obstacle to the young Scot who is, in many cases, receptive to spoken Scots but not to written Scots.

These facts about Scottish literature we regard not as insuperable barriers but as challenges requiring the teacher to consider his methods as carefully as he would for the successful handling of any other demanding text, whatever its origins. In particular, we would resist any suggestion that these facts combine to render Scottish texts in some sense 'irrelevant', or that any text should be rejected because it fails to meet some narrow criterion of contemporary relevance. The mediation of an interested teacher can educate pupils into a generous and imaginative sense of what is relevant and if vitality of language and concentration on an illumination of some aspects of human behaviour or experience is present in Scottish texts, we consider it sufficient reason for proffering them to Scottish pupils in a Scottish classroom in the twentieth century.

There can be no simple formula to resolve the problem of how much Scottish literature to use and how much time to devote to it. The English Department must decide for itself in the light of its particular circumstances, but such decisions should not be made in ignorance of 'what is there, what is not there and what could be there'.

# The Early Stages

Since the publication in 1967 of the Central Committee's Bulletin No. 1 (*English in the Secondary School: Early Stages*) valuable work has been done in developing courses for the early stages which emphasise the production of oral and written work rather than the direct appreciation of works of literature. In urging here the contribution that literature, and in particular Scottish literature, can make we are not suggesting that the Bulletins have ignored its importance. Indeed Bulletins Nos. 1 and 2 deal with the text-based curriculum at some length, with reference to what they call the Second Stage of pupils' development, and even in their discussion of the First Stage with its emphasis on projects they recognise the value of poems and stories in the classroom, and of recreational reading at home. Nevertheless, we feel it worthwhile to reaffirm that, in the words of the Banffshire working party, 'It is wrong to concentrate so much on asking pupils to express themselves and produce creative work that too little time is left for them to meet and feed on the ideas and experience of others.'*

We are not contradicting the fundamental insights of the Bulletins. They stress '*doing* rather than *contemplating*: speaking, writing and reading for specific practical purposes with short term goals' and their preferred mode of learning is the project which provides a context for this work. Such an emphasis is not at odds with the use of literature. The exploration of a text is entirely consistent with the philosophy of active learning; and, of course, every good story or poem creates its own 'context'— its own imagined world.

For many pupils, the early stages of the secondary school will provide their first substantial contact with Scottish literature, and we would emphasise that this initial contact should be pleasurable. Fortunately, Scottish literature, we believe, abounds in attractive material likely to appeal to our younger pupils. The choice that we make will be made on the criteria that would be used for any reading material. It will be, in the main, short and self-contained. It will be written in language that is direct and vivid in its appeal to the imagination. It will deal with matters within the emotional and cognitive grasp of the children who will read it. It will work through the particular, the concrete, the specific rather than the abstract and general. It will deal with genuine human situations (which does not mean that it will be solemn). Any programme of such reading will be varied containing story, poem and drama and different kinds within each genre. It should lend itself to variety in treatment by class and teacher.

*\*English for Mixed Ability Classes in the Common Course*, Keith, 1974.

The aim of the 'treatment' is always the same: to enable young readers to develop their skill in taking meaning from the text as they read it or hear it. This is no narrow aim, for good literature (and all that that phrase means in this context is satisfying stories, exciting dramas, stimulating poetry) is that kind of writing in which men and women most seriously try to explore their own experience for themselves (and consequently for others) and in so doing reveal, consciously or unconsciously, how they conceive of themselves, what they value, what they think it means to be human. This is the kind of 'meaning' that children learn to take from the literature they read.

Because 'meaning' is conceived in this way, the importance of a distinctively Scottish component in our children's reading becomes evident. Through meeting, in the stories and poems and plays that they read, the attitudes and values, the doubts and certainties, the sources of compassion and cruelty, of humour and sorrow of their fellow Scots, young readers begin to acquire a sense of their own identity as it has been shaped by their own inherited culture.

But there need be no self-conscious 'teaching' to such an end. All that is needed is that the literature should be explored so that its meaning is grasped as fully as possible; and then it will do its own work.

Sometimes the approach should be through discussion, with the teacher leading the whole class; sometimes by discussion in small groups with the teacher being referred to only occasionally; such discussion may at times be based on a set of questions, fully formulated in advance, at other times quite free. The exploration may sometimes be done through singing a song or choral speaking of a poem; or it may be by dramatising the story or illustrating the theme. The exploration of the text may be by personal expressive writing arising from it and with which it may be compared. Finally, the treatment may be simply reading and listening.

At this early stage we would wish to employ a broad definition of literature which would encompass not only those generally accepted genres such as poetry, novels, stories and plays, but also such things as folk-songs, folk-tales and legends, historical material, newspaper reports and other documentary sources such as old photographs and drawings. In particular we would urge teachers to exploit the local: to use local place names, stories, traditions, local dialects, texts which deal with the area or with a clearly similar locality, local newspapers and other documentary materials. While such a local study might relate to work on History, Geography or Modern Studies and while it might use much the same kind of materials as these subjects and indeed benefit from the resources collected by local teachers of these subjects, we should be clear that the English teacher's interest will be primarily in the *imaginative* exploration of historical events or the use that can be made in the pupils' writing of features of the local environment. It is only fair to recognise of course that some localities have more to offer than others, that some are richer in local literature than others, but most areas have considerable untapped potential which the teacher might consider using.

It should be borne in mind that good local material has always more than mere local significance and that therefore even if a locality appears to be bereft of resources for this kind of study, search will very often produce valuable material dealing with parallel situations in other localities.

These general considerations justify the use of literature in a wide variety of ways: from the teacher's reading of a short story or poem and leaving it at that, through the close exploration of a text by one of the several modes we have mentioned, to the using of a group of related texts clustered together because they illumine each other, or some topic or some theme. In what follows we make suggestions that cover such a range.

## Poetry

We feel it appropriate that our younger pupils (and we include primary pupils) should be allowed some opportunity to explore the phenomena of the Scots language as the raw material of poetry. Such pupils have not yet passed beyond the stage when they find these fascinating and amusing in themselves:

'What the child, and the child-in-the-adult, most enjoys in poetry is the manipulation of language for its own sake, the sound and rhythm of words.'*

Chambers's one volume *Scots Dictionary* (eds. A. Warrack and W. Grant, 1911), the local Street Map and Telephone Directory, a Gazetteer and the appropriate One Inch Ordnance Survey map are all useful resources in bringing pupils to investigate and enjoy the sound and sense of family names, street names, place names and local idioms and pronunciations. Such simple investigations offer the opportunity for small research projects in the language of the individual, the family, the class, the school and the community. (See 'Words, Alive, Alive-O', P. J. McLaughlin, *Teaching English*, Vol. 8, No. 1 for the methodology of a language investigation at primary level using cassette recorders.) It is important to stress that these language explorations are not likely to be limited in their appeal to the ablest pupils only.

A related area of study that we recommend for younger pupils is what William Soutar called bairn-rhymes. As Robert Chambers, the Montgomeries, the Opies and the School of Scottish Studies have abundantly demonstrated, Scotland is quite exceptionally rich in both the number and lyric quality of its popular rhymes— street songs, play rhymes, riddles, traditional festival rhymes, tongue-twisters, place rhymes, weather rhymes, epitaphs, curses and spells, work rhymes and proverbs. The pleasure and the importance of these embryonic literary forms is not to be underestimated.

'A language is learned and a culture planted in childhood. So these rhymes should precede the pleasure derived from hearing the more mature ballads and folk-songs. Indeed the fundamental quality of these rhymes attunes the young ear to all poetry.'†

Pupils should be encouraged to contribute, tape and anthologise their own local collections of such materials. (It may be possible, for instance, for them to visit old people's organisations in search of examples.)

Music for some of the best known Scottish bairn rhymes is to be found in the appendix to *101 Scottish Songs*.**

The initiative of the B.B.C. *Scottish Magazine* series in exploiting the possibilities of this traditional lore is greatly to be welcomed, and its related magazine, printing as it does both programme material and pupils' contributions, is a development of great potential value to teachers.

The range of Scottish poetry at our disposal should encourage the variety of approach particularly desirable with younger pupils. Ballads, songs and laments, satires and humorous narratives, poems in English and Scots, modern concrete poems—all of these offer different opportunities for discussion, for singing, for choral speaking, illustration, dramatisation, writing or simply for reading and listening. The treatment of each individual poem will be determined not by any preconceived notions of what should be done but by the unique nature of the work of literature in question.

* W. H. Auden: *A Choice of de la Mare's Verse*, Faber, 1963.
† N. & W. Montgomerie: *The Hogarth Book of Scottish Nursery Rhymes*, Hogarth, 1964.
**N. Buchan: *101 Scottish Songs*, Collins, 1962.

At the time of writing there are no adequate collections of Scottish verse for the early stages. But the material exists, abundantly, for the interested teacher who is prepared to search. Some of the texts will be contemporary but we urge a consideration of the whole time span, from the current *Akros* and *Lines Review* back to *The Bruce*, and including the folk contributions of *Tocher*. In selection we favour catholicity and width of sympathies, an eye for what will really go with children, rather than for the slogans of Scottish literary battlefields. In this connection we recommend some reconsideration of the modest but genuine talents of the later Kailyard—of writers such as Walter Wingate, David Rorie, Joe Corrie, W. D. Cocker, Andrew Dodds and Joseph Lee. At their best these are poets of wit and compassion, writing directly out of their own experience and commanding a fluent colloquial Scots style.

We are particularly fortunate in having the resources of ballad poetry at our disposal. Our traditional ballads are, of course, more than merely versified stories, but it is their narrative power which principally commends them to the teacher working with the early stages. They have the advantages that they are widely anthologised and that sung versions are readily available on records and cassettes (see Bibliography pp. 107–109).

As narratives they are attractive for many reasons. They range widely in mood—tragic, comic, fantastic, eerie, brutal, romantic and heroic. They deal with elemental matters which are still very much with us: a search through a few days' newspapers will throw up abundance of situations worthy to be the subject of original balladmaking. At the same time, after sampling a few ballads, pupils can be brought to recognise that there is a definable ballad 'world', an imaginative world apart, in which certain types of people, objects, events and attitudes tend to recur. Some teachers, indeed, have found it profitable to develop an imaginary community project out of the typical characters and events of the ballad world—the cattle thief, the eloping daughter, the bereaved mother, the rhymer—and so on. However, we are not suggesting that ballads be read in order to collect typical features: their value as material for younger pupils may indeed have been minimised in the past by a premature concern with classification—an excessively literary emphasis on ballad stanzas, rhyme schemes and the listing of typical language features.

Our main purpose is to endorse the wisdom of the long-established practice of offering ballads as good stories. A nucleus of about a dozen of the greatest of these ballads (e.g. 'Sir Patrick Spens', 'The Wife of Usher's Well', 'The Twa Corbies', 'The Battle of Otterbourne', etc.) has for long been widely, and justly, popular in Scottish schools, but we would suggest a more adventurous investigation of the full ballad canon. At a rough estimate, some fifty of the ballads in the *Oxford Book* (ed. J. Kinsley, 1969) are probably usable in one way or another.

Moreover, whilst recognising that the singing style of the traditional ballad singer may sound bizarre and outlandish to young ears attuned to other harmonies, we nonetheless urge the use, wherever possible, of sung versions of the ballads. The English teacher's interests are not antiquarian and he should consider the whole range of available versions, from Jeannie Robertson to The Corries and Steeleye Span.

Dramatisation of ballads in class is a popular method of treatment, but it is difficult to handle and success often eludes even the most careful preparation. Burlesque is sometimes the unintended result, and comic ballads are the ones most likely to succeed. Perhaps the surest way of dramatising ballads is by getting the pupils to prepare a radio script for tape-recording.

Certain ballads have one foot, at least, in history—e.g. 'The Battle of Harlaw', 'The Battle of Otterbourne', 'The Bonny Earl of Moray', 'Kinmont Willie'. Where a straightforward account is available (for example the story of the Kinmont Willie escapade is told in *The Steel Bonnets* by G. M. Fraser, pp. 291–293) we recommend a pairing of prose and verse, fact and myth.

Ballads may be interestingly grouped in clusters—e.g. those dealing with the lurid goings-on of certain powerful Scottish families:

*The Armstrongs*: Kinmont Willie, Johnnie Armstrong, Jock o' the Side, Archie of Ca'field

*The Gordons*: Edom o' Gordon, The Battle of Corrichie, Glenlogie, The Fire of Frendraught, The Baron of Brackley.

Or again, a ballad may be the core text for a range of work.

Examples:

(a) *Thomas the Rhymer*
True Thomas
Some of the prophecies and curses of Thomas of Erceldoune (in *Popular Rhymes of Scotland*, Robert Chambers, Edinburgh, 1841)
Act I of *The Lass wi' the Muckle Mou* by Alexander Reid
Dick o' the Cow (a good example of a 'Riding' ballad)
*True Thomas the Rhymer and other Tales*, T. & H. Scott, O.U.P.

(b) *The Seals*
The Selchie of Sule Skerry
Johnnie Croy and the Mermaid: N. & W. Montgomerie (*The Well at the World's End*)
The Goodwife of Wastness: H. Aitken (*A Forgotten Heritage*)
Macodrum's Seal Wife: (translated from Gaelic) *Tocher* Vol. 8, pp. 259–263
*Seven for the Sea*: W. T. Cutt, Andre Deutsch, 1972

(c) *Tam Lin*
Tam Lin
Tamlane: ed. J. Jacobs (*English Fairy Tales*, Bodley Head, 1968)
*Tamlane*: Anne Rundle, Hutchinson, 1970
Look also at the other, very different, folk hero, the fantastical bumpkin Tam o' the Linn (*The New Scots Reader*, ed. McMillan, Oliver and Boyd, 1973). In one of his Irish folk-song incarnations, Brian o' Lynn, he appears in *Scotch and Irish* (Robin Hall and Jimmie MacGregor, Decca LK 4601). Can these two Tams be the same person? Is there any connection detectable at all?

While we recognise that attempts to use poems in association with other material or as stimuli for various types of writing or drama work run the risk of distorting or detracting from the impact of the individual work, we nevertheless believe that, given tact and common sense, poems can profitably be 'presented' and 'exploited' with younger pupils.

An interesting set of suggestions for ballad work is, for example, contained in *English in Secondary 1*, the report of a Renfrewshire Working Party (1974), summarised in an article ('Beyond the Bulletins') by Brian Boyd and James Doherty in *Teaching English* Vol. 8, No. 2 (January 1975). A similar range of work might be constructed on other ballads.

To take a rather more recent narrative poem, 'Flannan Isle' might be offered as the culmination of an examination of contemporary documentation of the Flannan Isle accident of 1900.

The documents might be read and discussed in class in the following order:

(a) Public notice intimating the commencement of the Flannan Light.

(b) Telegram from the Master of the tender, Hesperus.

(c) Letter from Assistant Keeper, Moore.

(d) Lighthouse Superintendent's Report.

(e) Public statement by the Northern Lighthouse Board.

(All of these documents are to be found in *The Flannan Isle File* by Lanarkshire County English Committee, 1974, available from library of C.I.T.E.).

'Flannan Isle' by W. W. Gibson can be read and treated *as a poem*. The documentation will, among other things, place the pupils in the position of the writer, before he wrote his poem. This puts them in an excellent position to appreciate the nature of his achievement.* The study might conclude with a reading of Neil Gunn's account of a visit to the Flannan Isle, 'The Light that Failed' (*Highland Pack*, Faber, 1949). Is there in this any evidence that Gunn had read the poem?

By concentrating on the ballads we do not wish to suggest that there is no other Scottish narrative verse worth considering. But what has been suggested above will also apply to most other Scottish material of this type: to narrative folk song (e.g. Macpherson's Rant, Johnnie Cope, The Bonnie Lass o' Fyvie, The Barnyards o' Delgaty, The Hot Asphalt, Rothesay-O); and also to the works of the major Scottish poets who have essayed narrative, and who were heavily under traditional influences (e.g. Burns, Hogg, Scott, Stevenson, Soutar).

Contemporary poets have tended on the whole to avoid direct story telling but the following narratives are worth attempting with younger pupils:

The Combat (Edwin Muir) *Twelve Modern Scottish Poets*
I'm Neutral (Robert Garioch) *Contemporary Scottish Verse*
Responsibility (Norman MacCaig) *The Scottish Literary Revival*
A-a-all the Starboard Watch (J. K. Annand) *Two Voices*
The Ross-shire Hills (MacDiarmid) *Contemporary Scottish Verse*
Black Friday (James Copeland) *Contemporary Scottish Verse*
Hamnavoe Market (Mackay Brown) *Contemporary Scottish Verse*
Witch (Mackay Brown) *Fishermen with Ploughs*
Ae Nicht at Amulree (William Soutar) *Twelve Modern Scottish Poets*
The Whistle (Charles Murray) *New Scots Reader*
Glasgow 5 March 1971 (Edwin Morgan) *Worlds*
The Tryst (William Soutar) *Voices of Our Kind*
Ba Cottage (Andrew Young) *Complete Poems*

Of the non-narrative lyric verse which is frequently tried with younger pupils two classes can be singled out for special mention. The first of these is the very large group of 'animal' poems to be found in Scottish literature. Even ignoring the narrative fables we have a wealth of material, ranging from humorous 18th century elegies such as 'The Ewie wi' the Crookit Horn' (Skinner) and the 'Wee Freenly Dugs' of the Kailyard (cf. W. D. Cocker and Hilton Brown) to the bairnsangs of William Soutar, Sandy Thomas Ross, and J. K. Annand and the sophisticated inscapes of Muir, MacCaig and Morgan.

A smaller, rather more difficult class of lyrics is that which attempts without the

---

*Contemporary documentation of events from which literary works have grown can often best be found with the help of the local library, most of which carry back numbers of local newspapers. Nearly all national newspapers provide a service of photocopying and reducing whole pages of newsprint. From these master copies, excellent overhead projector transparencies can be made. It is of course necessary to give a precise date reference in making the request. Charges vary, but are in the region of 25p per page.

aid of narrative to present human characters, either depicting 'types' or evoking individual personalities. Many of the best of these are too demanding for younger pupils (e.g. 'Holy Willie's Prayer', 'Docken afore his Peers' by Charles Murray, or 'Old Woman' by I. Crichton Smith) but there remains enough to provide an attractive portrait gallery on a limited scale—more women than men, more old than young, more rural than urban:

An Auld Maid in the Garret *101 Scottish Songs*
Jean Calder (J. C. Milne) *Poems*
Tae the Beggin *101 Scottish Songs*
To Suffie (Flora Garry) *Bennygoak and other Poems*
Fishermen (Robin Munro) *Shetland Like the World*
Cophetua (Hugh MacDiarmid) *Selected Poems*
Uncle Roderick (Norman MacCaig) *A Man in My Position*
The O-Filler (Alastair Reid) *Passwords*
Our Big Beenie (Robert Garioch) *Selected Poems*
Grandpa (James Rankin) *Scottish Poetry 2*
Catherine (Sydney Tremayne) *Scottish Poetry 4*
For My Grandmother Knitting (Liz Lochhead) *Memo for Spring*
Sunday Bus (James Aitchison) *Sounds before Sleep*
There's Aye a Something (Charles Murray) *The Last Poems*

## Drama

In the field of scripted drama, Scottish literature has less to offer pupils of this age. Certainly there are some good one-act plays, and the teacher who is interested and knowledgeable in this field can find some eminently suitable extracts from plays which would not, in their entirety, be appropriate. In any case, much of the drama work done at this stage depends on improvisation rather than on script, or on scripting by the children themselves rather than by a playwright. Here we would merely refer to the opportunities offered for this kind of activity by Scottish poetry and tales, and indeed by the everyday realities of Scottish life. And if in their reading and in their classwork the pupils are made aware of the potentialities inherent in the Scots language, their dramatic improvisation and written scripts should benefit accordingly. (See Bibliography pp. 80–82, and also comments on Drama in the Section on the Older Non-Academic Pupil.)

## Prose

In prose as in poetry the material and the approach will be varied. Here again much of what will appeal to the young comes from the past, from the store of traditional tales and legends and from the wealth of historical anecdote in which our literature abounds. Many of these stories exist in several versions. The Bibliography under 'Stories and Legends' (p. 98) gives examples of what is available. Paperback editions exist for many of the titles.

The teacher with a talent for story-telling (as distinct from reading) will find this an effective approach; otherwise he should take care to select that version which reads most naturally and effectively. The stories lend themselves to dramatisation; they are useful models of short narrative; they provide through discussion a way into the minds of their original creators. (Even the most rationally resistant twelve-year old can be challenged with the questions: why should these tales have been told at all—what can you learn about their authors and their original hearers—what kind of picture of the world did they have?)

Professional historians have for years criticised Scottish education for what they tend to regard as its 'Tales of a Grandfather' approach to the national past. 'Perhaps it is typical of a small country,' writes Rosalind Mitchison, 'that there should be a wide gulf between the opinions of the current generation of working scholars and the popularly held truisms about its history.' Modern Scottish school history, as typified in the excellent series 'Then and There' (Longman) and 'History for Young Scots' by Cameron (Oliver and Boyd), goes a long way to meet these strictures. But the transmutation of fact into fable is itself an inevitable part of the historical process. The hero tales of Scotland (from Cuchullin, Calgacus, Columba, Magnus, Wallace, Bruce, Douglas through Mary, Knox, Montrose, Charles Edward to Burns, Watt, Livingstone, Fleming, Logie Baird . . .)—these may comprise as much romance as history but they are enthralling in themselves and have a great deal to reveal of the history that Scots would *like to have*. Educationally nothing but good can come from the collaboration of history teachers and English teachers in helping younger pupils to see the fact and the fable side by side.

## Non-Fiction

For such pupils the strong appeal of non-fiction prose as leisure reading is a fact easily documented by reference to school library borrowings. Biographies, topographical and travel writing, sport, out-of-door activities, natural history, popular history—where available, Scottish examples of all of these should find a place on the junior shelves. We provide suggestions in our bibliographies (pp. 94–103).

For class work, valuable selections of prose extracts of Scottish interest have been available in the recent past in the pioneering collections *Scottish Harvest* and *Scots Adventuring* (McPhedran and Kitchen, 1960 and 1961). We see scope for additional contemporary anthologies of this type. Given adequate reprographic facilities the interested teacher can find much of interest for class use in Scottish newspaper and magazine journalism.

The study 'Fox and Wildcat' is offered as an illustration of the deployment of a set of relatively short prose texts for younger pupils (Appendix).

## Short Stories

There are unfortunately few Scottish short stories written specifically for children, though a number of stories for this stage can be found in general collections and anthologies. One such, 'The Kitten' by Alexander Reid, is used as the core text of the unit 'Fox and Wildcat' offered as an exemplar (Appendix). We also recommend for example the following:

> The Sea Cook (Neil Munro) *Para Handy Tales*, Pan, 1969
> Dandy Jim the Packman (John and Jean Lang) *Scottish Harvest*, McPhedran and Kitchen, Blackie, 1960
> Portrait of a Footballer (Morley Jamieson) *The Old Wife and Other Stories*, M. Macdonald, 1972
> Touch and Go! (David Toulmin) *Hard Shining Corn*, Impulse Books, 1972
> Tartan (G. Mackay Brown) *A Time to Keep*, Hogarth, 1969
> Black Andy's Tale (or Tod Lapraik) (R. L. Stevenson) *Scottish Harvest*
> Alicky's Watch (Fred Urquhart) *Scottish Short Stories*, Urquhart, Faber
> The Mennans (Robert MacLellan) *Scottish Short Stories*, Urquhart, Faber
> The Gray Wolf (George Macdonald) *Scottish Short Stories*, Reid, O.U.P., 1963

The dialect element in some of the stories in the above list will make considerable demands on the resourcefulness of the teacher as a dramatic reader. But we believe that the skills involved are well worth developing since lively story reading, even when only one copy of the text is available, is a most beneficial activity with younger pupils.

The B.B.C. has recently offered useful support in this area and we particularly commend such fine professional performances as Bryden Murdoch's rendering of 'How the Sabistans Came to Orkney' by George Mackay Brown.

## Children's Novels

As the Bibliography suggests (pp. 90–93) there is a wide range of good quality fiction for young readers set in Scotland. It is desirable that the school library be generously stocked with these works and pupils encouraged to consider them as interesting recreational reading (the importance of which was so strongly stressed in Bulletin No. 1).

The novel is not particularly easy to handle as a class text but many teachers do so with success and some of the works of writers such as A. C. McLean, Honor Arundel, Iona McGregor are worth using as class or group readers. The methodology of the unit study as discussed, for example, by R. D. Jackson in *Teaching English* Vol. 7, No. 3 and Vol. 8, No. 1 may be considered.

What follows below is a possible study linking a relatively recent novel with a classic of children's fiction.

*Heroes and Villains*

1. *Texts:*

   Allan Campbell McLean, *Master of Morgana*, Collins Armada Lions, 1974
   Robert Louis Stevenson, *Treasure Island*
   These texts are paired because they are both sea adventure stories which centre on a boy's relationship with an ambivalent adult hero-villain. The parallel between the works is close and explicit. The 'Master of Morgana' is a salmon fisher, Long John MacGregor, 'a sea-faring man . . . with only the one leg'. Early in the book one of the characters compares him with 'the fellow in the story, Long John Silver'. Throughout, McLean deliberately re-works Stevenson's material.

2. Several arrangements of the material are possible. What is suggested here is a study of the *Master of Morgana* culminating in the reading of *Treasure Island*. Conceivably the emphasis might be reversed, or an attempt made to tackle both books concurrently exploiting, step-by-step, opportunities for comparison and contrast.

   This study concentrates on one central aspect of *The Master of Morgana*, the personality of the hero-villain Long John. However, there are many other aspects of the book that might be explored, for example:

   (a) McLean's story is very firmly localised. A place and way of life are finely exploited as background. Using Bartholemew's Half Inch map of Skye and Wester Ross the pupils can trace the action in some detail.

   (b) The crofting, fishing way of life can be examined. In *Explore the Highlands and Islands*, H.I.D.B., 1973, pp. 16–17, McLean is clearly describing the same setting used in his novel.

   (c) The attitude of Niall to all the women folk is worth looking at.

   (d) The Gaelic-English idiom of the characters is a feature of interest. Why, for example, does the Factor sneer at Niall (p. 36) when he says, 'I was working the outboard on my brother's boat since years.'

   (e) How convincing are the policemen and the part they play in the story?

3. *Suggested Treatment*

    (a) Introductory double period. Read and discuss Chapter 1 in class.

*Writing Assignments:*

Personal account of domestic crisis, illness, accident.

Report of Ruairidh's accident such as might appear next day in local paper.

    (b) Allow class a week to complete reading of novel—at home or with a period or two of silent reading in class.

    (c) Then follows a set of 8–10 periods spread over two or three weeks, preferably double periods devoted to examination of certain key situations in novel.

| | | |
|---|---|---|
| Passage 1 | First appearance of Long John | pp. 46–50 |
| Passage 2 | Long John at work | pp. 55–58 |
| Passage 3 | Long John and the knife | pp. 124–133 |
| Passage 4 | Long John's past life | pp. 136–138 |
| Passage 5 | Niall discovers the truth | pp. 173–179 |
| Passage 6 | The last of Long John | pp. 190–192 |

For each of these sessions there should be some preparatory re-reading of the episode in question, given point by one or two questions. Discuss the episode in class and use it for a variety of oral and written assignments, for example:

Passage 1    A boy starting his first job. Compose a dialogue between the boy and his boss. Describe Niall as he might appear to Long John.

Passage 2    A factual description of the stages of the salmon fishing. Explain Niall's comment (p. 58) 'Some cripple, I thought.'

Passage 3    Make an acting episode out of the events described on pp. 132–133.

Passage 4    Develop in writing one of the episodes of Long John's past, e.g. the time that the cook got drunk, the time that he lost his leg, the time that he first used the harpoon gun.

             Suppose that Long John is looking for a new job. Write the outline of his working life that he might give in a letter of application.

Passage 5    Tape the dialogue between Niall and Long John:
'Well you beat me in the end . . .'
'Mind you bolt the door' (pp. 174–179)
Write the charge that the police might make against Long John on the evidence of his confession, pp. 174–179.

Passage 6    What will happen to Long John and Kingfisher out on the Sound of Raasay in the fog (p. 192)? Write a final chapter to the story as epilogue.

    (d) Read the opening pages of *Treasure Island* to the class and give pupils a fortnight to read it at home.

    (e) *Final assignment*

Write a comparison of the two Long Johns.

## Clusters

So far we have been principally concerned with the use of individual texts, or with several texts from one genre clustered together. Clearly, however, it is possible and desirable to use Scottish texts as the basis for, or as an important element in, projects that have a literary basis, or in thematic work. We use the term 'cluster' loosely, to cover the sort of work in which a variety of texts are used to throw light on one another, or on some topic or theme. The methodology of such work often describes the literature used as 'input', a term which has the effect of making us anticipate an 'output'. It is as well to remember, however, that there *need* be no manifest 'output' in the form of writing or tape recordings (or drawings and painting). A varied reading experience that results in reflection and thoughtful discussion needs no further justification. We offer in varying detail suggested texts for the following clusters: (a) local, (b) historical, (c) supernatural, (d) domestic, (e) animal. The particular groupings we suggest here and elsewhere are intended as no more than examples of the kind of thing that can be done, and we would hope that teachers would experiment with their own selection and organisation of material.

*Local*
Of necessity, copies of local texts are likely to be hard to come by, but single copies can usually be consulted through the local library service and brief extracts may normally be photocopied relatively cheaply. What follows is a cluster centred on two nineteenth century works famous in their time but now little known. They are strictly local in reference, but are of considerable human interest and, in extracts, eminently suitable for younger pupils. Moreover, the subject with which they deal, flood disaster, can be made to widen into contemporary relevance.

During two days in August 1829, the whole North East of Scotland, from the River Nairn to the South Esk, was ravaged by flooding of unparalleled ferocity. The physical and human consequences of the disaster were systematically chronicled by Sir Thomas Dick Lauder in his minor prose classic *The Moray Floods* (3rd Edition, 1873). This contains vivid first-hand, dialect accounts of their experiences by victims of the floods, for example:

Chapter 4, pp. 69–70, The Findhorn, and Isabella Morrison
Chapter 18, pp. 149–151, The Spey at Orton, and John Geddes
Chapter 21, pp. 170–173, The Flooding of Banff
Chapter 24, pp. 194–198, The Dee at Ballater

The effects of these same floods upon animals and men at Feughside and the Forest of Birse are recounted in vigorous and entertaining episodic Scots verse in 'The Muckle Spate of Twenty-Nine' by David Grant (*Lays and Legends of the North*, 1884). Episodes that might be used:

'The cadger body, Johnny Joss'
'The Tollman at the Brig o' Feugh'
'The Dog o' Gellan'

In addition to extracts from these two texts, a cluster on *Flooding* might utilise other local material.

(a) A collection of N.E. river and weather rhymes. (*Notes on the Folklore of the North-East of Scotland*, Rev. Walter Gregor, 1881).

(b) Information about local traces and evidence of the 1829 floods still visible.

(c) Landseer's great sentimental narrative canvas in Aberdeen Art Gallery, 'Flood in the Highlands'. (Postcard prints are obtainable from the Gallery or, locally, pupils might visit the Gallery.)

(d) David Rorie's comic verses:
The Lum Hat wantin a Croon (with music, in *101 Scottish Songs* ed. Buchan, 1962)
Tinkler Pate (in *The Lum Hat wantin a Croon and other Poems*, Rorie, 1935)

Developing from the local, one might introduce W. D. Cocker's version on the Noah theme 'Ballad of the Deluge' and recommend as recreational reading the following non-Scottish, children's novels:

*Flood Warning*, Paul Berna, Puffin
*Hill's End*, Ivan Southall, Puffin

A serious contemporary dimension can be supplied by a consideration of contemporary disasters such as those of Honduras and Bangladesh.

*Historical*

In History many younger pupils work with *Scotland in the Time of Wallace and Bruce* by W. K. Ritchie in Longman's 'Then and There' series. This sets the military adventures of Wallace and Bruce simply and vividly in the context of the social, economic and political history of their times, and is aptly illustrated. The narrative sections are themselves good examples of story-telling, providing occasional short extracts from Barbour in modernised verse.

From the following texts material might be selected to expand the imaginative aspects of this study:

*Tales of King Robert the Bruce*, T. Scott, Pergamon
(a prose version of *The Bruce* that keeps close to Barbour's narrative)

The Ballads of 'Gude Wallace' and 'Sir William Wallace'
(in *Scottish Ballad Poetry* ed. G. Eyre-Todd or *English and Scottish Popular Ballads* eds. Sargent and Kittredge)

*Tales of a Grandfather*, Sir Walter Scott
(Chapter VII: 'The Story of Sir William Wallace': episodes of Wallace and the trout, Hazelrigg, The Barns of Ayr, Cressingham and Stirling Bridge)

With reference to Ritchie: *Scotland in the Time of Wallace and Bruce*,

Chapter 1: 'Michael Scott and the Witch' (in *A Forgotten Heritage* ed. Aitken)
'How Michael Scott went to Rome' (in *Scottish Folk Tales and Legends*, ed. Wilson)

Chapter 2: 'Oscar and the Giant', 'Finn and the Gray Dog', 'Rashie Coat', 'The Wee Bannock', 'Whippity Stourie' (all in *The Well at the World's End*, ed. Montgomerie, N. and W.)
Ballads of 'The Wee Wee Man', 'Tam Lin', 'Alison Gross', 'True Thomas'
'The Statue in the Hills' (G. Mackay Brown)
'Smooring Prayer' (in *Tocher*, 1, p. 9)

Chapter 3: Act I of *The World's Wonder* by Alexander Reid
*The Head* by D. K. Haynes

Chapter 4: 'The Twa Corbies'
The 'Thomas the Rhymer' material previously mentioned in connection with the use of ballads.

The period is dealt with in the following historical novels suitable for children:

*Alexander the Glorious*, Jane Oliver
*Young Man with a Sword*, Jane Oliver
*The Lion is Come*, Jane Oliver
*Ransom for a Knight*, Barbara L. Picard

Extracts from Nigel Tranter's Bruce trilogy may also be found useful.

*Supernatural*

Wandering Willie's Tale, Letter XI, *Redgauntlet*, Scott
Story of Robin Ruthven and the Minister, *Private Memoirs and Confessions of a Justified Sinner*, Hogg
Story of Tibbie Johnston by Hogg (in *Garland of Scottish Prose*, Mackenzie)
Kilmeny, Witch's Song, etc. by Hogg
The Carl of the Kellyburnbraes
Tam Lin
Thomas the Rhymer
The Fause Knight
The Wee Wee Man
The Strange Visitor
Clerk Saunders
The Demon Lover
The Wife of Usher's Well
Alison Gross
Tam o' Shanter (Burns)
Address to the De'il (Burns)
Thrummy Cap (John Burness)
The Last Night (Stevenson) *Dr Jekyll and Mr Hyde*
Thrawn Janet (Stevenson) *The Merry Men and other Tales*
Tod Lapraik (Stevenson) *Catriona*
What the Moon Saw (Buchan) *Witchwood*, Chapter 8
The Outgoing of the Tide (Buchan) *The Watcher by the Threshold*
The Black Officer of Glaick (Calum McLean) *The Highlands*, Chapter IV
The Dundee Ghost (Matt McGinn)

Numerous folk tales in *Tocher*, *Scottish Folk Tales and Legends* (B. K. Wilson), *The Highlands and their Legends* (O. Swire), *The Well at the World's End* (N. and W. Montgomerie), *A Forgotten Heritage* (H. Aitken), *Gaelic Ghosts* (S. Nic Leodhas). See also some of the stories in *The Clans of Darkness* (Haining).

*Domestic*

A cluster of texts on the subject of family life:

Poems: Get Up and Bar the Door, Binnorie, Edward, Lord Randal, The Twa Brothers, The Philosophic Taed (Soutar), The Deil o' Bogie (A. Gray), The Two Parents (MacDiarmid), For My Grandmother Knitting (L. Lochhead), Aunt Julia (MacCaig)

Prose: extracts from *The Taste of Too Much* (Hanley), *Morning Tide* and *Highland River* (Gunn), *The Last Summer* (I. Crichton Smith), *House of Elrig* (Maxwell), *Autobiography* (Muir), children's novels by Honor Arundel.

*Animal*

We present, finally, a more detailed working out of a programme of work based on a cluster of texts about animals. This programme and its related literature is to be found in the Appendix.

# Scottish Literature and the Older Non-Academic Pupil

The appreciation of literature in schools implies a basic literacy in pupils. Even if, in the present context, Scottish literature is taken to include a comprehensive range of textual, verbal, and pictorial items having Scottish elements in form and/or content, important variables affect the teacher's selection of material. Degrees of reading skill and linguistic ability impose constraints, and it is generally acknowledged that receptiveness and response are notably volatile commodities in this area. Nevertheless, Scottish literature—as distinct from other literatures—merits serious consideration, since it has a special contribution to make in providing local material of direct relevance to the needs and interests of older non-academic pupils.

Since the raising of the school leaving age and the extension of Ordinary SCE examination gradings, presentations in English have been increased by the inclusion of candidates from the upper reaches of the group referred to. For these pupils, any fuller awareness of literary values and corresponding development in language skills is less likely to stem from prospective examination presentation or formal lessons on Scot. Lit., than from the engagement of their minds, imaginations and emotions through a continuing dialogue between themselves and their teachers.

It may be, however, that some of the suggestions made in the 'Scottish Literature in the Fourth and Fifth Years' section of this report should be considered—with modifications where necessary—as applicable to them. Scottish folk-songs, in particular, might be extensively explored. Since not all teachers of English are likely to have made wide use of folk-song, it may be of value to outline some possible advantages. It would be unrealistic to ignore the fact that teachers often encounter, at best, apathy in trying to interest non-academic pupils in poetry in any form, Scots or English. Folk-tunes, in themselves, are in many cases sufficiently near to an acceptable modern musical idiom, or compulsive enough in their rhythms, to bring the classroom audience to the point where some consideration of the lyrics is possible. Again, examples may be found in a humorous vein sufficiently unsophisticated for pupils to respond to (e.g. 'Skyscraper Wean' and 'The stoutest man in the Forty-Twa'). There may also be a case to be made for the preparation of overhead transparencies of the poems with illustrations in order to achieve a variation from the more formal poetry book approach. Folk-songs are of interest and value in themselves, and they can help pupils to overcome whatever prejudice they may have against classroom poetry.

Since songs mentioned in this section have been recorded on discs and cassettes, and since the words of many may be found in printed collections,* pupils may be able to participate directly by supplying their own items for class use. Where local items can be found, they have an added appeal in being *local*, a consideration which cannot be too strongly emphasised in the selection of *all* Scottish material, of whatever *genre*, for this category of pupil. At the same time, it is not suggested that only Scottish items should be used. Scottish folk-music bears comparison with that of any other country and should, where possible, be set alongside examples from elsewhere.

A possible area of interest, for which a wide range of folk-song illustrations can be found, is occupations. Many of these songs provide revealing commentaries on work-experience and job-status, from the irreverent 'Fa' wid be a Bobby?' and 'My Brither Bill's a fireman bold' to 'The Keltie Clippie', a mock-romantic serenade to the Lily o' Lumphinnans. There is scope also for exploration of soldiering, an occupation followed by Scots in every generation. Many pupils have relatives and friends who follow the trade of armed peace-keeping, and many boys regard the army as a possible career for themselves. Folk-songs express a variety of attitudes. There is the simple and direct heroism of 'Jamie Foyers'. There is the realism, the admission of the darker side of soldiering, in 'The Braes of Killiecrankie'. There is the swagger and bravado of 'Johnny Cope'. There is the unashamed patriotism of 'Scots Wha Hae'. There is self-mockery in 'The stoutest man in the Forty-Twa'. Many moving songs, like 'The Bonnie Lass of Fyvie', dealing with inevitable partings, derive from the rootlessness of the soldier's life. Even in meretricious and over-romanticised songs like 'There was a soldier', 'Here's tae the Gordons' and 'Have ye seen the Cameronians?' there still exists the opportunity to examine the appeal of soldiering.

If a more extended study of the above topic is proposed, some of the following sources might be appropriate. Alexander Scott's poem 'The Sodgers' (*Twelve Modern Scottish Poets* ed. C. King: p. 144) shows that donning a uniform does not necessarily create a taste for soldiering; and some of the bleaker realities encountered by the 'sweirt sodgers' may be discovered in the extract from Lewis Grassic Gibbon's *Sunset Song*, in which Chae Strachan, home on leave from the trenches in World War I, tells Chris Guthrie why her husband, Ewan, came to be shot as a deserter. Further comments might be provided by some of the following: the English version of Sorley Maclean's 'Death Valley' (*The Scottish Literary Revival* ed. G. Bruce, p. 72) or, where feasible, the Gaelic original (op. cit. 'Glaic a' Bhais', p. 71); Walter Wingate's 'After' (*Scottish Verse 1851–1951*, p. 128); extracts from George M. Fraser's *The General Danced at Dawn* (Pan, 1974) and/or *McAuslan in the Rough* (Pan, 1974); Neil McCallum's *Journey with a Pistol* (Gollancz, 1959) (extract describing looting on Mount Akarit, pp. 108–110, and the final episode, the battle for Sferro in Sicily, pp. 156–160); episodes involving Richard Hannay's encounters with the 'Fusilier Jock', Geordie Hamilton, in Buchan's *Mr Standfast* (Chapters IV, VIII, and XII). For this topic there should be no lack of audio-visual illustrative material.

So far in this section consideration has been given, in the main, to pupils in the upper ranges of the non-academic. Nevertheless, the claims of the less able are not to be disregarded, however formidable the difficulties appear†.

Many of these pupils will have a reading problem which may, by this stage, have created an armour-plated reluctance to contemplate reading for pleasure. For those whose reading difficulties require remedial assistance, considerable ingenuity has

---

*e.g. *The Scottish Folksinger*: eds. N. Buchan and P. Hall (Collins, 1973) and *Personal choice of Scottish Folksongs and Ballads*: Ewan MacColl (Hargail Music Press, New York).

†'... it is important that every effort be made to make these opportunities available to pupils who cannot find them for themselves. As with the very young, so with the older non-academic pupils the teacher must seek every means possible to make the maturing influence of literature accessible to them'. C.C.E. Bulletin No. 2, p. 25: *The Teaching of Literature*, H.M.S.O. 1968.

already been deployed in producing texts specifically designed to help them improve their performance levels, though Scottish elements do not bulk large in this material. There is a promising field for experiment in the use of drama scripts with poorer readers. Written to be spoken aloud, the dialogue makes for easier reading, while sympathetic identification with characters in problem situations can improve motivation to master word-recognition and meaningful expression. Greater confidence in verbal self-expression, in which many young Scots appear deficient when compared with their contemporaries in other parts of the British Isles, might also be encouraged by this practice. It is to be hoped that, should this method of developing reading skills gain currency, drama scripts with Scottish language elements would be produced, since, as C.C.E. Bulletin No. 3* claims, 'such pupils respond best . . . to texts written in styles near to the everyday usage familiar to them'.

For pupils whose reading skills are more developed but not yet at levels which would permit them to read rapidly and with enjoyment the children's fiction with Scottish backgrounds listed elsewhere in this report (pp. 90–93), there is a dearth of Scottish material for private and recreational reading. Modern stories, in simple language, with plots derived from contemporary life and its problems, and told in terms of young people with whom readers of this kind can identify, are being written and published especially for this age group and ability level. While Midland and North of England *milieux* are frequent in these, Scottish ones are not. The fault here may lie with Scottish authors in neglecting this market. Publishers might be persuaded to see in Scottish stories the lure of the exotic for southerners and the appeal of the familiar for the native born. There is scope also for the introduction of a Scottish component in multi-media kits, such as *Situations* (Blackie), currently being produced for use by less able pupils.

Where the printed page imposes a barrier to interest and enjoyment, pupils who take little pleasure in reading a story may still have their imaginations caught and held when listening to one. Scottish history and legend, local and national, and Scottish folk-lore, urban and rural, contain an abundance of colourfully mysterious and macabre tales. The Great Grey Man of Ben Macdhui, the capital's Major Weir, Deacon Brodie and Burke and Hare, Glasgow's Madeleine Smith and Dr Pritchard: these are only a few examples in a *genre* that lends itself to spoken narrative. While stories of this kind may be read to the class from books, with the teacher adapting the language where necessary to the understanding of the class, it may be more effective for highlighting elements in the story and to prevent interest flagging because of detail and length if the teacher narrates it in his own words. Sensational 'human interest' stories are not confined to the domain of legend and folk-lore. Sawney Bean and his family, or the Mad Son of the Duke of Queensberry,† may be no more than footnotes to the annals of vanished ages, but stories of this kind are still the life-blood of modern tabloid newspapers, and it is not so long ago since survivors of an air crash in the Andes brought necrophagy back to their pages. A topical news item could be used as an introduction for this type of narrative and could give opportunities for language work on translating an old story into modern journalistic idiom.

A further approach to the development of listening skills can be made by playback of tape recordings of Scottish stories broadcast in schools programmes and elsewhere. By this means pupils may hear Scots well spoken and in a variety of dialects not always within the competence of the individual teacher to reproduce accurately. This method of presentation has the additional merit of demonstrating to pupils that the Scots language has a vigour and range of effects peculiar to itself as well as a field of native or vernacular options unsurpassed in any other English-speaking region. Here

*English for the Young School Leaver, H.M.S.O. 1970, p. 13.
†See Scottish Tales of Terror ed. Angus Campbell, p. 13.

also may be found at least a partial answer to linguistic difficulties which may affect teacher and pupils alike in Highland areas where Lowland idioms and lexis are unfamiliar. Tom Leonard's cryptic miniatures of Glasgow *patois* ('wee burdnma wurk then/nutsnur a wuz'*) may strike a responsive chord in Coatbridge or Castle-milk once the phonetic spelling has been appreciated, but there may be no such ease of communication in classrooms in Oban or Inverness. If the teacher feels uncertain of doing full justice to Lowland sounds and intonations—a feeling perhaps shared in Lowland areas where texts from the North-East are concerned—the use of recorded material could provide an approach, particularly in verse, which would extend the field of study beyond the relatively local. It should be noted, however, that, in using tape-recordings with pupils whose listening span is limited, careful consideration should be given to the length of playback the class can accept without the loss of concentration. Longer stories will almost certainly have to be serialised. If, however, the teacher is prepared to keep a sharp eye on advance programme details and to ensure that recording arrangements are made, a valuable sound anthology can be assembled. Short stories recorded on cassettes are beginning to appear on the market: in due course Scottish ones may appear.

While the primary purposes of narration may be to engage the imagination, develop listening skills and spark off verbal responses, narrative can also provide a starting point for creative work and explorations in other media in collaboration with other departments. Many examples of interdisciplinary activities may be found among projects undertaken over the last decade in connection with the Saltire Study Scheme. A brief selection from those graded 'outstanding' includes *The Witches of Borrowstounnes*, incorporating a dramatisation of a witchcraft trial; *Escapade: A Tale of Tillie-Tudlem*, a film scripted, costumed and acted by pupils; and *The Battle of Largs*, illustrated by a relief model 33 ft. by 9 ft. in area. A current Saltire Society leaflet lists twenty-four suggestions for future projects of which the following would involve literary and linguistic studies: 'Life and Character in . . .' (tales, jokes and pictures of worthies of the town, district or county; end product: a book); '. . . in the days of . . .' (an account of the district as it was known by a famous past inhabitant—e.g. Scott, Burns, Barrie, etc.; end product: a book); 'A literary map of the local area' (e.g. Burns Country, the Borders, the Mearns: identifying areas to which the author refers, allying scenes with quotations; illustrating scenes; comparing contemporary and modern depictions of the scenes; end product: exhibition of maps, paintings, pictures *or* a book); 'The language of the area' (Do the pupils speak English or Scots? A comparison of local vocabulary and phrases and standard English: local pronunciation and received English; end product: a book of essays or a vocabulary list or a phonetic study); 'A dramatic reconstruction' of historical events associated with a local ancient monument; (end product: a performance *or* pageant *or* book). Non-academic pupils have made significant contributions to the Saltire Study Scheme in the past, and while the projects mentioned above imply a measure of local history research, there are many others listed in the pamphlet referred to in which the contemporary scene may be explored. These also can include an element of literary study.

Included in the exemplars† to accompany this section of the report, there is a local study which applies to an area in the North-East. It is offered as a model of a type which could be effective in any area and which gives scope for out-of-school activities. This approach affords opportunities to invite local experts and specialists to come into schools and provide pupils with first-hand information on the topic being studied. It is in this context, also, that the relevance of literary material can be made most obvious to pupils.

*from 'Yon night' by Tom Leonard, *Akros* Vol. 9, no. 27.
†Available from C.I.T.E. (see page (iv)).

Some teachers of English in urban areas may not previously have explored the possibilities of local studies and may feel that such activities can more easily and profitably be pursued in a rural context. There may be some truth in this, but contemporary writers have become increasingly preoccupied with the rapid and radical changes in urban life-styles and the loss—for good or ill—of much that gave identity to individual towns and cities. There would seem to be a strong case to be made for trying to ensure that those pupils who are least likely to take note of change and its implications for urban communities should have their attention drawn to significant elements in town life in the immediate past to help them to a heightened awareness of the perplexities and complexities of the present.

The song, 'Where is the Glasgow where I used to stey?' could open an investigation of the changes which have taken place in the way of life of young people in Glasgow within a generation and of the problems which progress has brought in its wake. The third verse contains a ready-made questionnaire to test on today's teenagers the extent of the decline of games and *patois* once familiar to their parents. How many could accurately gloss the questions posed in:

'And where is the wean that once played in the street
Wi' a jorrie, a peerie, a gird wi' a cleek?
Can he still catch a hudgie an' dreep aff a dyke,
Or is writing on walls noo the wan thing he likes?
Can he tell Chuckie Mellie frae Hunch, Cuddy, Hunch?'

*The Scottish Folksinger* contains the text (with a glossary for those who may require it).

Briefly dealt with, G. S. Fraser's 'Lean Street' (*Penguin Book of Scottish Verse*, p. 480) might supply an astringent corrective to the over-simplifications of nostalgic reminiscence before turning again to the lighter side of growing up in a tenement as described by Cliff Hanley in 'A Breathless Hush in the Close Tonight' (from *Dancing in the Streets*) or the threat of (pre-)adolescent anarchy to beleagured respectability voiced in Stephen Mulrine's 'The Coming of the Wee Malkies'. The transition from the togetherness of tenement life to the alienation of high-rise flats can be managed by a recording of 'Skyscraper Wean'. Slums may be too great a price to pay for sociability, but comfort and cleanliness cannot entirely compensate for the loss of companionship and conviviality. There is a general feeling that high-rise flats may have solved some social problems only to create new ones. The class might well consider how they affect the lives of mothers, young children, teenagers, old people. 'Clydesdale New Town Talk' by Duncan Glen, and 'Cougait Revisited' by Donald Campbell (both to be found in *Made in Scotland*: ed. Robert Garioch, Carcanet Press, 1974) may also be of interest for this topic.

Though more difficult, with its raw alliterative Lallans indignation ('Hidderie–hetterie stouteran in a dozie dwam/O ramsh reid-biddie') and its close-packed imagery, Sydney Goodsir Smith's 'The grace of God and the meth drinker' (*Twelve Modern Scottish Poets*, pp. 113/114) could also be included with some classes for its angry compassion for the human derelicts that town planning and social welfare have as yet failed to rehabilitate. In this vein there is also 'Man o' the warld' by Donald Campbell (in *Rhymes and Reasons*, Reprographia, 1972). Or again on a lighter note, Stephen Mulrine's 'Nostalgie' (*Scottish Poetry 6*: Edinburgh University Press) is a companion piece for 'Where is the Glasgow where I used to stey?' and opens up avenues for discussion which might be extended to include other instruments of social change, especially the exploitation of North Sea oil resources. Additional suggestions for urban studies, outlined in greater detail, are contained in the exemplars already referred to on page 23.

Profitable areas of interest in which complementary non-literary material and activities can be incorporated are also to be found in the field of occupations. Two of these—mining and fishing—suggest themselves as being suitable for extended study both from the abundance of material available, and in respect of certain aspects of the occupations themselves. They have common features in that those who follow them help to produce the means to satisfy basic human needs—warmth and food. While they are not unchanged by the advances of modern technology, they still clearly demonstrate the importance of the human factor, and because of this are a fruitful source of literary material. Something of the dangers and discomforts, the occupational hazards, and the economic importance of these industries can be studied in terms of the *mystique* of physical endurance and human skills which go hand-in-hand with a deep-seated traditionalism and pride in doing a hard job.

For mining, suggested texts are: Joe Corrie's play, 'Hewers of Coal' (*Five Scottish One-Act Plays*, ed. Millar and Low); extracts from Iona MacGregor's *The Burning Hill* (Faber) which deals with earlier inhuman practices in eighteenth century serf-mining; stories from Charles Brister's *This is my Kingdom* (David Winter & Son, Dundee, 1972). Mining songs can be found in *The Shuttle and Cage* (Hargail Press, New York) and in A. L. Lloyd's *Come all ye bold miners* and *Coaldust Ballads*. Two useful poems by Joe Corrie are 'Miners' Wives' and 'Image O' God' (*Penguin Book of Scottish Verse*, pp. 456 and 457), while W. S. Graham has an interesting comment to make in 'Fourth Sonnet' (1940) (in *The Ring of Words*) in which the 'whisky-balanced miner' on the bus 'Brings through his pit-hoarse voice his lea-rig heart'. Complementary material from English and Welsh sources, as well as suggestions for the development of this area of interest in non-literary ways, can be found in *Area Resource Centre: An Experiment* by Emmeline Garnett (E. Arnold, 1972: Chapter 5, Mines, Mining and Miners). Illustrative material and films are not difficult to come by. Best of all, if it can be arranged (N.C.B. officials are invariably helpful here), is a class visit to a coal face.

A study of the fishing industry presents similar opportunities for a multi-activity project. Anyone who can lay hands on a copy of the record, 'Singing the Fishing— A Radio Ballad' (Argo DA142)* should find it of value for introducing this topic. This documentary by Charles Parker and Ewan MacColl is a mixture of folk-songs and recorded reminiscences of the herring fishing industry earlier in the century by men and women from East Anglia and the North-East of Scotland. Suitable prose texts may be selected from Neil Gunn's *The Silver Darlings* (for example, the story of the voyage in Chapters 14 and 15) (see Novel List), J. MacDougall Hay's *Gillespie* (see Novel list) (Chapters 8 and 9 give an interesting insight into the economics of fishing and may suggest simple research topics), and stories from George Mackay Brown's *A Time to Keep* (see Short Stories: Individual Authors list). Many poems deal with fishing, and examples are to be found in most anthologies. They vary in difficulty, but careful selection can afford means of illustrating a number of view-points; from Sydney Goodsir Smith's 'Whan yon lane boat I see/Daith and rebellion blinn ma ee!' ('Largo': *Twelve Modern Scottish Poets*, p. 108), via George Campbell Hay's 'a man with a boat of his own, and a mind to guide her' ('To a Certain Loch Fyne Fisherman Who Keeps to the Old Ways': *Ring of Words*, p. 54), to George Mackay Brown's 'Twelve cold mouths scream without sound' ('Haddock Fishermen': *Twelve Modern Scottish Poets*, pp. 164/165). As in the case of mining, there should be no great difficulty in finding illustrative material connected with fishing. The White Fish Authority and the Herring Industry Board are useful sources. It may be possible to arrange a screening of John Grierson's famous early documentary, 'Drifters' (Central Office of Information). Visits to a fishing harbour or fish processing factories

*There is also a film of an updated television version.

may also be possible. For those within travelling distance, there is the Fisheries Museum at Anstruther. Of interest to girls would be *A Taste of Scotland in Food and Pictures* by Theodora Fitzgibbon (Pan Books) which contains a number of recipes appropriate to this topic. In addition, a useful collection of short items on the sea and fishing (some by schoolchildren) is contained in BBC Scotland's *Scottish Magazine* No. 2 (December 1974).

Additional material, which might have been included in the two studies dealt with above, could be retained for use, with other items, in a shorter theme on public disasters. Concerned with a mining tragedy, there is the song, 'The Donibristle Disaster' and another on 'The Auchengeich Disaster', while 'The Shira Dam' recalls the hardships and loss of life in the building of a hydro-electric scheme. Losses incurred in the fishing industry are commented on in two poems by George Mackay Brown, 'Unlucky Boat' (*The Ring of Words*, p. 121) and 'Warped Boat' (*Twelve Modern Scottish Poets*, p. 160). Parts of the central narrative section of Hugh MacDiarmid's 'The Wreck of the Swan', and William McGonagall's 'The Wreck of the Whaler Oscar' are other possible sources for sea disasters. The local area may also provide material for study on this topic. The Tay Bridge disaster is the subject of a well known poem by McGonagall and an account of it appears in A. J. Cronin's *Hatter's Castle* (extract in *Scottish Harvest*, Blackie, p. 79). The serious rail disaster which occurred at Gretna during the first World War had unusual legal implications since the train straddled the border when the accident took place. Few pupils would fail to appreciate the cruel irony of the returning servicemen drowned when the s.s. 'Iolaire' sank outside Stornoway Harbour on New Year's Eve, 1919.

Sport as a topic may have more appeal for boys than for girls, and while no suggestions are made for extended study, it might be of interest, where boys' classes are concerned, to read and discuss short prose extracts and poems on this topic. An appreciation of Tom Leonard's poem 'Fireworks'* (*Akros*, Vol. 9, No. 25) might be achieved by setting alongside a tape-recorded extract from a match commentary. More literary sources for football extracts are *The Thistle and the Grail* by Robin Jenkins and *From Scenes Like These* by Gordon Williams, and such poems as 'Fi'baw in the Street' by Robert Garioch (*Selected Poems*), 'Rythm' by Iain Crichton Smith (*The Ring of Words*) and 'Tynecastle' by Donald Campbell (*Rhymes and Reasons*, Reprographia, 1972). Tom Leonard's 'Yon Night' (*Akros* Vol. 9, No. 27) presents a cameo of double despair from a big match defeat and female apathy ('hoffa mi wuz greetnaboot Celtic/anhoffa mi wuz greetnaboot hur').

The development of field studies and adventure centres has given many young Scots of all ability levels some knowledge of Scotland's mountains. This interest could be encouraged by the reading of extracts from Alastair Borthwick's *Always a Little Further* (Smith, 1961), W. H. Murray's *Mountaineering in Scotland* (Dent, 1966), Dougal Haston's *In High Places* (Cassell, 1973), and Tom Patey's *One Man's Mountains* (Gollancz, 1971). There are interesting and informative articles by W. H. Murray and Tom Weir in back numbers of the *Scots Magazine*. These suggestions for textual material on various topics are intended to allow a selection to be made to suit various ability levels.

The drama script offers a most effective means of contact with the imaginative resources of the less able. Mention has already been made of its potential as a means of encouraging poor readers. Their phrasing, speech rhythms, and timing improve with practice, and the feeling behind the words has a more dynamic context in which to emerge. Dramatic dialogue commands more attentive listening than does a

*'up cumzthi wee man
  beats three men
  slingzowra crackir . . .'

reading of extended prose or verse passages. Above all, given the blueprint of dialogue, the pupil can imaginatively identify with a character in conflict with himself or circumstances and can thereby vicariously widen his experience of life.

This is not to claim that, even with all these advantages, drama scripts will be easy reading for non-academic pupils. An effective script is a highly compressed account of a fragment of living containing within itself an evaluation of that living. To realise its full meaning it is necessary to 'read between the lines', tease out ellipses, concentrate on short scenes. It is, however, the very nature of the drama script that makes this kind of attention to the text feasible in a way that is hardly practicable with other forms of literature. Since the drama script is unrealised theatre, the teacher can prompt exploration of its meaning by asking 'production' questions: What tone of voice would you use for that line? Where would you be looking as you say that? Paradoxically, the more closely the text is studied in this way, the *less* academic the activity becomes. The pupils, moreover, can respond in a range of ways: by movement, gesture, intonation. They are freed, in fact, to explore and to express meaning in ways that they find much more sympathetic than the abstract and formal language that school often demands of them.

A major difficulty here, however, is that there are few Scottish drama texts available in editions prepared for classroom use. Until there is a more general appreciation of the value of native scripted drama, there are several sources of material that can be investigated. A range of good, dramatic Scottish one-act plays is in print, but available only in paperback acting editions. Their appeal has been proved on the amateur stage and many of them are generally popular with the community at large. A selection of them could provide a commentary on Scottish humour in all its varieties. Robert McLellan's *The Changeling* (W. Maclellan, 1951) is a highly amusing version of the sheep-stealing scene from one of the cycles of English mystery plays retold against a background of the Scottish Borders in the early seventeenth century; *Jeddart Justice* (see Bibliog. Drama: Short Plays) by the same author dramatises the story of the lass wi' the muckle mou'; civic dignitaries of Glasgow are involved in a slightly macabre but Gilbertian situation in T. M. Watson's *Hangman's Noose* (Brown, Son and Ferguson); the tribulations of an amorous and Falstaffian Ayrshire J.P. provide the comedy in Elizabeth Milne's *The Cracket Joug* (Brown, Son and Ferguson); John McCabe's *The Friars of Berwick* (see Bibliog. Drama: Short Plays) is a mediaeval romp, entertaining both in incident and dialogue: the list could be continued at length. For those who care to explore this virtually untapped reserve of Scottish drama, there are no doubt reading sets in Scottish Community Drama Association libraries in various cities throughout the country. Local drama clubs may also have sets which they might be prepared to make available on loan.

An alternative is to experiment with extracts from longer plays. If the school possesses a set of James Bridie's *The Anatomist* for the use of the general sixth, it could with advantage be borrowed for fourth year classes. The two scenes of the second act are virtually self-contained, include some of Bridie's finest vernacular writing, alternate the comic and the macabre without losing the appearance of truth to life, and yet can hardly fail to make an impact on the least imaginative of pupils. The first scene of Act I of Bridie's *A Sleeping Clergyman* contains parts which could be equally effective. Contemporary Scottish drama is becoming increasingly available in printed form. Extracts from, for instance, *Willie Rough* and *The Bevellers*, could also be selected for this approach.

Further experiments can be made in the field of drama using radio plays. Taped broadcasts of plays by Scottish authors offer scope for the examination of a neglected but not negligible dramatic form. The successful radio play—which may have a running time of thirty minutes (for weekday broadcasts), one hour (Friday afternoons) or one and a half hours (Saturday Night Theatre: repeated Monday afternoons)*—must have general appeal and make an immediate impact on listeners of all intellectual levels. It is tightly constructed, has a logically developed story-line, undemanding language, and provides a concise exposition of a contemporary problem in human terms. Its construction in short scenes affords scope for simple analysis of dramatic structure. If it is tape-recorded, analysis is simplified, and so it has an advantage over television drama (at least until video-recording becomes general), and, with sound only, the listener acts the drama 'in the theatre of his own mind'.

For creative expression, radio drama offers a model within the capabilities of all but the least able. From a preliminary outline of scenes, a play to be taped can be built up line by line on the blackboard with the teacher filling in scraps of dialogue when communal invention flags. Ideas for dramatic structure and method can be borrowed from a stage play such as *The Cheviot, the Stag and the Black, Black Oil* (West Highland Publishing Company, 1974). Ballads, local history and legends, many with highly dramatic incidents and colourful characters, can supply an abundance of plot outlines.

Radio plays require sound effects which call for ingenuity and experiment if they are to be convincing. Music 'bridges' between scenes provide opportunities for critical listening and selection from records (Scottish instrumental music could be useful here), or for instrumental contributions from pupils, even if only simple percussion. And above all, the team-work required for a successful final recording can effect a high degree of group concentration as a climax to what has been throughout a corporate activity.

*Plays on Radio 3 may be any length and are not selected for their mass-appeal potential.

# Fourth and Fifth Years

In this section we are concerned with those pupils in fourth and fifth year for whom a text based course is appropriate. That is not to say that they form a homogeneous group. At one end of the ability range there are those who will leave school at the end of their fourth year with a C pass in Ordinary Grade English; at the other end, there are those who at the end of their fifth year will be looking forward to English at C.S.Y.S. level. Clearly, within this range, the teacher has to cater for a variety of needs and abilities when designing literature programmes, selecting texts and considering methods of presentation. It is, however, broadly true that, in spite of these differences, the level of maturity and command of reading skills possessed by pupils at this stage means that the teacher is largely freed from those restraints on the choice of texts which we have noted in earlier sections. This means that a very wide range of Scottish literature is now available to the English Department which wishes to make use of it.

This freedom in the selection of texts generally, and in the selection of Scottish texts in particular is in no way circumscribed by the demands of the S.C.E.E.B., for both the Ordinary and Higher examinations allow the English Department to organise the kind of literature programme which it deems appropriate to the pupils for which it has responsibility.

The principles and methods of literature teaching have been dealt with at length in previous C.C.E. Bulletins.* These principles have, we believe, found general acceptance among English teachers, and the methods outlined there are widely practised. It is not our intention to cover this ground again. We have agreed, however, that in planning and organising a literature course, the teacher of English in Scotland should include a substantial element of Scottish literature. What we offer in this section, therefore, are some practical suggestions about the kind of texts suitable at this stage, and about ways in which they can be fruitfully grouped together or incorporated into the overall English programme. The ways in which the teacher uses Scottish texts will not differ significantly from the ways in which he uses any other texts. Some poems, stories and novels he will want to study on their own, for their own sake, because they have something significant and valuable to say to his pupils. Some texts, he may find, will benefit from juxtaposition with others, and this might involve the pairing of Scottish texts with those from other literatures, or the comparison of

*Bulletin No. 2 *The Teaching of Literature.*
 Bulletin No. 4 *English in the Secondary School: Later Stages.*

contemporary and traditional Scottish material. Or the texts might form part of more elaborate thematic groupings of the kind illustrated in some detail in the exemplars in Bulletin No. 4.* In certain areas, such as Edinburgh or Glasgow or the Highlands, the teacher might wish to make use of texts with local associations: we have suggested this as a valuable tactic in the earlier stages, and it would be no less effective with more sophisticated texts and more mature pupils. With older and abler pupils the teacher might wish to embark on the study of a genre or of the work of an individual author. In what follows we suggest some examples of all of these approaches. Moreover, the section on the General Sixth follows essentially this pattern and, since there can be no hard and fast line dividing those materials suitable for S4 and S5 from those suitable for the non-S.Y.S. Sixth, the teacher may find some of the specific suggestions about texts in that section applicable to fourth and fifth year classes.

In selecting Scottish material for use in the classroom, the teacher will have to bear in mind certain considerations. As with all texts he will, of course, consider the needs, interests and abilities of his pupils, and the need to present them with a balanced literature programme. In addition to these general considerations, however, the teacher using Scottish literature will want to take advantage of the opportunities (particularly in the area of linguistic variety) offered by the interaction of Scottish and non-Scottish materials and by the comparison of texts in different styles and from different regions within Scotland itself.

### Poetry

Scottish poetry has never been entirely neglected in fourth and fifth years. The ballads and some poems of Burns have always found a place, and an anthology like *Poets' Quair* has for many years offered the enthusiast the possibility of looking at such poets as Dunbar, Henryson, Fergusson and MacDiarmid.

We have already suggested that the ballads can provide useful material for younger classes than those we are considering here. Such is the nature of the ballads, and the wealth and variety of the material available, however, that their use with younger pupils is not incompatible with a more mature study of the genre at this stage. The approach can vary. Although too scholarly an approach to variant forms would be inappropriate, the comparison of two versions of a ballad (e.g. the versions of 'Lord Randal' in *Poets' Quair* and Robert Graves's *English and Scottish Ballads*) can lead pupils to make value judgements and examine the basis of such judgements. (Which is the better version, and why?)

Child provides a virtually inexhaustible mine of such material, though most teachers would not feel it necessary for the purposes of close study to go beyond the best-known ballads.

Moreover, a number of ballads are readily available on record, so this process of critical evaluation can be extended from the printed page to a consideration of performance. A wide range of contrasting styles is available to the teacher. Consider, as a sample, 'The Child Ballads I' (12T160 Volume 4),† 'The Child Ballads II' (12T161 Volume 5),† A. L. Lloyd and Ewan MacColl's 'English and Scottish Folk Ballads' (12T103),† the American folk singer Joan Baez's version of 'Mary Hamilton' in 'Joan Baez on Vanguard' (SVXL 100), The Corries' performance of 'The Twa Corbies' in 'Kishmul's Galley (STL 5465) and Steeleye Span's treatment of 'Alison Gross' in 'Parcel of Rogues' (Chrysalis Records). An approach of this kind to the ballads through variation, comparison and recorded performance might specially appeal to the less literary-minded fourth year pupils, and might be linked to a study

*Bulletin No. 4 *English in the Secondary School: The Later Stages.*
†Topic Records.

30

of other kinds of Scottish folk song which share with the ballads the major themes of love, marriage and death.

Like the ballads, the poems of Burns are appropriate at more than one level in the school. Some, certainly, like 'Holy Willie's Prayer', 'The Holy Fair' and 'The Twa Dogs' demand maturity and some knowledge of the social and religious background of the time. Such poems are, perhaps, best kept till fifth year, but there are others perfectly suitable for fourth year pupils. 'Tam o' Shanter', of course, is a proved favourite. 'The Address to the Unco' Guid', 'The Address to the Deil' and 'A Man's a Man for a' That' prepare the way for a later look at the religious and social satires. 'To a Louse' has plenty of linguistic vigour and humour. 'To a Mouse' is an effective and moving poem in its own right, and a comparison between it and 'To a Mountain Daisy' could lead to the beginning of an understanding of some of the conflicting forces operating on Burns. Then there are the songs which form such an important part of his poetic output. Much of Burns is available on record and while a poem like 'Holy Willie's Prayer', for example, might well gain from a professionally skilful reading, it is for the songs especially that the recordings are of value. Songs like 'Ae Fond Kiss', 'O Wert Thou in the Cauld Blast', 'Mary Morison' and 'A Red Red Rose' all have to be heard as well as read. The range and variety of tone and attitude in his songs is remarkable as one can see by comparing the rather melanchony ones listed above with such songs as 'Duncan Gray', 'O Whistle and I'll Come to ye, My Lad' and 'Willie Brewed a Peck o' Maut'.

Burns's poetic output was substantial and varied. It is important that pupils should be made aware of the wide range of his poetry encompassing narratives, dramatic monologues, satires, verse epistles and lyrics. It is important, too, that they should have some awareness of the social and religious background of his poems; this is especially important for an appreciation of the satires. And it is important that the teacher's approach to the poems should be varied. We have already suggested the use of records. Cartoon films illustrating readings of 'Tam o' Shanter' and 'Holy Willie's Prayer' are available for hire (see bibliography). While Burns is certainly a suitable subject for special study, there is every reason why his poems should be seen in a broader context, taken together with poems by other writers, Scots and English, of the past and of the present. A comparison of some of his love songs with modern popular love songs might appeal to less literary fourth year pupils. Poems such as 'Scots Wha Hae' and 'A Parcel of Rogues' could make a link with History teaching in the school or form part of an investigation of Scottish patriotism along with poems like Alexander Gray's 'Scotland', Edwin Muir's 'Scotland 1941' and 'Scotland's Winter', Hugh MacDiarmid's 'The Parrot Cry' (all in the *Penguin Book of Scottish Verse*), Edwin Morgan's 'The Flowers of Scotland' and the folk song of the same name by The Corries.

Any study of satirical poems should find a place for 'The Twa Dogs' and 'Holy Willie's Prayer' and the latter together with, say, Robert Garioch's 'Bingo, Saith the Lord' (*Scottish Poetry 5*) would provide useful points of comparison with some of Browning's dramatic monologues or with Betjeman's 'In Westminster Abbey'.

With a good fifth year class (with an eye, perhaps, to an interesting dissertation in C.S.Y.S.) some comparison could be made between Burns and Fergusson, between, for example, 'The Cotter's Saturday Night' and 'The Farmer's Ingle' or between 'The Holy Fair' and Fergusson's 'Hallow Fair' or 'Leith Races'. (For these and other suitable poems by Fergusson such as 'Braid Claith' and 'The Daft Days', see *Fergusson —A Bi-Centenary Handsel*.)

Rather more difficult (because of their language) than Burns or Fergusson are the other major poets of the past that we have mentioned, but while it is right to acknowledge the difficulties posed by Henryson and Dunbar, we would argue that our best pupils in fifth year should have some knowledge of them, of, say, Dunbar's 'Meditatioun in Winter' and 'Lament for the Makaris' and of Henryson's 'Tale of the Uponlandis Mouse and the Burgess Mouse' (all in the *Penguin Book of Scottish Verse*). Henryson, of course, is one of the authors specified for study in C.S.Y.S. and an introduction to his work in fifth year would be valuable.

The same is true of MacDiarmid and a number of his poems are well worth doing in fifth year or even earlier. Especially successful are some of the early lyrics from *Sangschaw* and *Penny Wheep* such as 'The Watergaw', 'Crowdieknowe', 'The Eemis Stane', 'Wheesht, Wheesht' and 'Empty Vessel' (all in the Penguin *Selected Poems*). Midnag publications (see bibliography) produce a strikingly effective poetry poster making use of his poem 'The Bonnie Broukit Bairn'. William Soutar's poems 'The Tryst', 'The Makar', 'Song' (all in the *Penguin Book of Scottish Verse*) and 'The Lanely Mune' and 'The Thocht' (both in *Modern Scottish Poetry*) make splendid companion pieces to these poems of MacDiarmid.

Opportunities to study works by these major poets have existed for some time and have been extended by the recent publication of inexpensive paperback selections of Henryson and MacDiarmid (see bibliography). Recently, the range of Scottish poetry, especially modern and contemporary poetry, easily available to the teacher has been increased by the publication of such anthologies as *The Ring of Words, Contemporary Scottish Verse, Twelve Modern Scottish Poets, Penguin Modern Poets No. 21* and *Worlds* (for further details see the poetry section of the bibliography). All of these will provide a large number of individual poems worth reading for their own sake in fourth and fifth year. The thematic organisation of *The Ring of Words* makes it a useful source book for teachers organising their work in that way. All the others allow the teacher to pursue with the class the further study of the work of a poet who has appealed to them.

Any suggestions we make here about poems and poets worth studying are very far from exhaustive. There is a wealth of material available, and the teacher will be guided not only by the nature of his class, but by his own tastes and preferences. There is, though, some evidence of the popularity in fourth year of poems such as Edwin Morgan's 'In the Snack Bar', and of 'Good Friday' and 'King Billy', Edwin Muir's 'The Horses', George MacBeth's 'Bedtime Story', Hugh MacDiarmid's 'Old Wife in High Spirits' (all in *The Ring of Words*) and James Copeland's 'Black Friday' (in *Contemporary Scottish Verse*).

It is important, though, that no narrow orthodoxy of 'suitable' poems should be established. There is certainly no reason to use a restricted range of poems. *The Ring of Words* for example, can supply, as well as those already mentioned, poems for this stage as varied and interesting as 'Hard Frost' by Andrew Young, 'Alas Poor Queen' by Marion Angus, 'Pride' by Violet Jacob, Albert Mackie's 'The Molecatcher', William McGonagall's 'The Destroying Angel', Ian Hamilton Finlay's 'Glasgow Beasts' and many others. Teachers in some areas might find useful the co-existence in *Contemporary Scottish Verse* of Gaelic and English verions of such poems as Sorley Maclean's 'Heroes' and Derick Thomson's 'Coffins' and 'Strathnaver'. In other areas, Joe Corrie's mining poems 'The Image o' God' and 'Miners' Wives' (both in the *Penguin Book of Scottish Verse*) might have a special relevance, and a teacher exploring War in a thematic study would find Sydney Goodsir Smith's 'Mither's Lament' and Alexander Scott's 'The Sodgers' in *Twelve Modern Scottish Poets*. Of the other anthologies listed in the bibliography those edited by George Bruce, Maurice Lindsay and Robert Garioch will all yield interesting material. The teacher who is prepared to look beyond anthologies to the works of individual authors might be rewarded by such gems as Robert Garioch's 'Fi'baw in the Street' (in his *Selected Poems*), and in Liz Lochhead's *Memo for Spring* he would find poems with a strong appeal to girls of this age such as 'A Poem for my Sister', 'Overheard by a Young Waitress' and 'Cloakroom'.

In fifth year, pupils are capable of benefiting from an even wider range of poems, some by poets we have already mentioned: Edwin Muir's 'The Castle' and 'One Foot in Eden', for example, Robert Garioch's 'Sisyphus' and Sydney Goodsir Smith's 'The Grace of God and the Meth Drinker' all in *Twelve Modern Scottish Poets*. This anthology will supply poems like Iain Crichton Smith's 'Old Woman' and 'Culloden and After', George Bruce's 'The Curtain', George Mackay Brown's 'Our Lady of the Waves' and 'The Hawk' and Norman MacCaig's 'Summer Farm', 'Byre' and 'Assisi'. Its arrangement (by poets rather than themes) allows the teacher to explore with a good class the work of a poet like George Mackay Brown, Norman MacCaig or Edwin Morgan. (In the case of the last two, he will find the Penguin anthology *Worlds* a very useful supplement.)

Some of Morgan's poems—the ones we have mentioned as suitable for fourth year and others such as 'Trio', 'Death in Duke Street' and some of his 'Glasgow Sonnets'—will have a special appeal in the Glasgow area (together, perhaps, with the work of poets like Tom Leonard and Stephen Mulrine). That his work has more than local interest, however, and an unusual range is shown by poems like 'Message Clear' (in *The Second Life*), his 'Computer' poems, 'The Fifth Gospel', 'Letters of Mr Lonelyhearts' and 'The First Men on Mercury' all from his collection *From Glasgow to Saturn* (the last poem incidentally makes a splendid companion piece to Ray Bradbury's story 'Dark They Were and Golden Eyed').

The remarkable fertility of imagery in some of MacCaig's poems such as 'Movements', 'Sounds of the Day', 'Laggandoan Harris' and 'Spate in Winter Midnight' makes him a particularly fruitful subject of study (though in his poem 'No Choice' he has said, 'I am growing, as I get older/to hate metaphor'). The combination of simplicity and subtlety in George Mackay Brown's work makes him both a popular and a rewarding poet at this stage. Pupils far removed from Orkney and the way of life he celebrates will respond to poems like 'Old Fisherman with Guitar', 'Haddock Fishermen' and 'Winter Bride' (all in *Twelve Modern Scottish Poets*).

The teacher need not feel himself confined to the poems and poets we have mentioned here. The anthologies listed in the bibliography will yield at least as many poems again suitable for studying at this stage, and if he feels it appropriate to study the work of one poet in greater detail with his class he will be guided by their response and interest which can as easily be stimulated by Liz Lochhead, Alan Jackson, Alasdair MacLean or Donald Campbell as by MacCaig, Crichton Smith or Mackay Brown. Teachers organising their literature teaching on thematic lines may find that the inclusion of Scottish poems can broaden and enrich a theme because of their distinctive Scottish point of view and, often because of the nature of the language. A study of poems on the theme of Love, for example, might benefit from the inclusion of some of Burns's songs, Sydney Goodsir Smith's 'Cokkils' and 'Elegy VIII' (*Twelve Modern Scottish Poets*), Alasdair MacLean's 'Question and Answer' (Contemporary Scottish Verse), Muriel Stewart's 'In the Orchard' (*Modern Scottish Poetry*), Liz Lochhead's 'Obituary' (*Memo for Spring*) and 'Today' (*Akros* Vol. 9 No. 25), and, though much more than a love poem, Sorley Maclean's 'Hallaig' (*Four Points of a Saltire*).

The size of the Scottish component in a theme will, as we have pointed out elsewhere, depend on a number of factors, but there could be times when it might be very substantial or even total. Consider the following grouping of texts which would occupy a good fifth year class for a considerable stretch of time, most of a term perhaps. The main prose text is Lewis Grassic Gibbon's *Cloud Howe* but as a preliminary (if it has not already been read) *Sunset Song* will be issued for private reading over a period of, say, three weeks. In the meantime some of the poems and short stories forming part of the theme can be studied. George Mackay Brown's short story 'A Treading of Grapes' (*Ten Modern Scottish Stories*) might make a good starting point, presenting a variety of religious attitudes as well as offering opportunities for work on language and style. His own poem 'Our Lady of the Waves' would develop one strand in the story, and Iain Crichton Smith's two poems, both entitled 'Old Woman' would develop another. The theme could be broadened by poems like Norman MacCaig's 'Assisi', Edwin Morgan's 'Fifth Gospel', Alastair Mackie's 'Vox Humana', Alexander Scott's 'Sabbath' and Sorley Maclean's 'Highland Woman' (Scots version in *Modern Scottish Poetry* and English version in *Honour'd Shade*). Before the class comes to study *Cloud Howe* it might read Gibbon's story 'Forsaken'. Other texts and a different arrangement might suggest themselves to teachers, but a good class having read these should have explored through discussion and writing something of the relationship between man, God and society. They will certainly have read some very worthwhile texts and been presented with an unusual variety of attitudes, styles, dialects and techniques.

*Short Stories and Novels*

Short stories are popular and useful teaching material at all stages in the school. They are, for the most part, of manageable length. They can be read purely for pleasure. They can be starting points for discussion and other oral or dramatic work. They can be stimuli and models for pupils' own writing. A teacher of a fourth or fifth year class will use them for all of these, but, in addition, he will want his pupils to have a greater critical awareness of the short story's distinctive features and techniques and he may wish to study with them the work of one of the short story's more interesting practitioners.

Scottish literature is not as rich in short stories as it is in poetry, and the number of collections suitable for classroom use is, unfortunately, limited. There are, however, some very fine Scottish short stories indeed, by major writers like Scott and Stevenson, by writers of the more immediate past like R. B. Cunninghame Graham, Neil Gunn and Lewis Grassic Gibbon, and by contemporary writers like Naomi Mitchison, Elspeth Davie, Eona Macnicol, Fred Urquhart, George Mackay Brown and Iain Crichton Smith. (The vigour of contemporary Scottish short story writing is illustrated by the publication in 1973 and 1974 of *Scottish Short Stories* by Collins and the Scottish Arts Council.)

These authors are by no means the only ones worth reading, but, even so, they present teacher and pupils with a wide range of subject matter and geographical background and a variety of styles and techniques. Scottish short stories will only be worth reading because they are good, of course, but this linguistic variety (often, but by no means exclusively lying in the use of dialect in dialogue) is an additional recommendation. If one of the teacher's aims is to sharpen his pupils' awareness of language variety and to encourage versatility and adventurousness in their own writing, then Scottish short stories can provide some invaluable source material.

Scott's 'Wandering Willie's Tale' and Stevenson's 'Thrawn Janet' (both in O.U.P. World's Classics *Scottish Short Stories*) are both worth a place in any study of the short story. They have in common that element of the macabre and the supernatural so common in Scottish folklore, and they are both firmly in the folk tradition of the 'told' story with a strong sense of the speaking voice and vigorous use of Scots in narrative as well as in dialogue. This same feeling for vigorous dialect speech pervading the whole story can be found in Lewis Grassic Gibbon's 'Smeddum' in the same anthology, a story in other ways very different from Scott's or Stevenson's.

These, and other stories by the same writers ('The Two Drovers', 'The Body

Snatchers', 'Clay') are all suitable for use with fourth year classes. So too (to take a random sample) are stories like Mackay Brown's 'The Whaler's Return', 'The Siege' by Elspeth Davie (*Spark and Other Stories*), 'Hurricane Jack' by Neil Munro (*Para Handy Tales*, Pan Books), 'Beattock for Moffat' by Cunninghame Graham (*Faber Book of Scottish Short Stories*), 'Flowers' by Robin Jenkins, 'The Bike' by Fred Urquhart and Iain Crichton Smith's 'Home' (all in *Ten Modern Scottish Stories*). These stories deal with many aspects of Scotland from Orkney to the Borders, but, more important than the incidental interest of locale is the fact that in their different ways they are all good stories. Para Handy's world may no longer exist but the stories are no less charming for that. Fred Urquhart's 'The Bike' for all its 20th Century urban setting belongs to a world as remote from the experience of our pupils as that of Wandering Willie's Covenanters or Mackay Brown's Norsemen, but it has at its heart a significant human experience (and is, in fact, an excellent springboard for discussion and personal writing). Where time and place coincide more closely with the pupils' experience (as they will for many in Iain Crichton Smith's 'Home') this will be an added attraction, a bonus, something the teacher can exploit as we have already suggested he can exploit the use of dialect in some stories.

The short stories we have mentioned are all suitable for fourth year classes, and indeed most of the Scottish short stories available would fall into that category. A teacher with a good class looking forward to fifth and even sixth year work, however, might consider the fact that there are some writers (and they are some of the best) whose short stories shed light on other aspects of their work. Scott and Stevenson are two such writers: 'Wandering Willie's Tale' could be a prelude to reading *Redgauntlet* in class or privately; Kirsty's tale of her brothers' revenge could be an introduction to the world of *Weir of Hermiston*. George Mackay Brown is an example of a modern writer exploring themes through poetry, the short story and the novel: while it would be wrong to look for points of detailed comparison, it might be fruitful to look at some poems and short stories together, perhaps in fourth year, certainly in fifth. Iain Crichton Smith is another: take for example, his novel *Consider the Lilies* and his poems dealing with old women in a West Highland setting; or compare *The Last Summer* with the stories in *Survival without Error*. We have already suggested the use of Gibbon's 'Forsaken' in a fifth year theme. Certainly any class going on to read *Sunset Song* would benefit from having read and discussed 'Clay' and 'Smeddum'. Clearly there are limitations to what can be done in this way in fourth and fifth year, but this linking of different aspects of a writer's work, valuable in itself, might possibly lead to further explorations in sixth year, perhaps in a C.S.Y.S. dissertation.

A number of Scottish novels have become established in fourth and fifth year literature courses in some schools in recent years. *Sunset Song*, the first part of Gibbon's trilogy is now widely used and is deservedly popular. *The House with the Green Shutters* is a powerful and compelling novel. Cliff Hanley's *The Taste of Too Much* makes a provocative and entertaining class text at fourth year level. Neil Gunn's *Silver Darlings* and *Highland River* (each in paperback) will both repay serious study, and will have additional appeal in some areas of the country. So too will Iain Crichton Smith's *Consider the Lilies* recently published in a schools edition. And *Weir of Hermiston* could be a revelation to pupils who only know Stevenson through *Treasure Island* and *Kidnapped*.

These are the novels most readily available in relatively inexpensive editions, and therefore the novels most commonly used as class readers. There are, however, a great many other novels just as suitable. They should, at the very least, be available in the library, and pupils should be given the opportunity and encouragement to read them.

Fourth year pupils would enjoy such books as *The Clearance* by Joan Lingard,

Allan Campbell McLean's *The Year of the Stranger*, Honor Arundel's *Emma* sequence (specially suitable for girls) and *The Popinjay* or *The Tree of Liberty* by Iona MacGregor. These are not difficult novels, most have a young person as protagonist, and all should appeal to the less literary pupils at this stage. Fifth year pupils should be encouraged to read as widely as possible in the field of adult fiction. Novels like *The Shipbuilders* by George Blake, *Tunes of Glory* by James Kennoway, *The Changeling* by Robin Jenkins, James Allan Ford's *Statue for a Public Place* and novels by Gordon Williams, Archie Hind and William McIlvanney should all appear in school libraries and on lists of recommended books.

Perhaps a special plea should be made for Scott, whose novels seem to have fallen into disfavour in schools (perhaps because, in the past, the wrong novels were pre-scribed for pupils too young to benefit from them). Most of the novels we have mentioned are contemporary or relatively modern. The advantages of using such texts will be obvious to most practising teachers, but, as we have already argued, the appeal of the contemporary is not in itself an argument for neglecting what is of value in the past. Much of Scott is of value. He is, after all, incomparably the best novelist Scotland has produced, and our best pupils in fifth year would most certainly benefit from reading his short stories and novels like *The Heart of Midlothian, Old Mortality* and *Redgauntlet*.

### Non-Fiction and Drama

To some pupils, non-fiction is more attractive than fiction. Some of these will be the less literary pupils in fourth and fifth year, but some will be abler pupils with special interests in, for example, Scottish wildlife or history or mountaineering. It is important that these interests should be catered for in the school or class library, and that pupils should be given every encouragement to read, talk and write about their enthusiasms. The non-fiction section of the bibliography offers some suggestions for suitable books under several headings, but this is a vast field, and the teacher or librarian will doubtless be able to augment this list from his own experience of what is popular and valuable.

Perhaps the major contribution of non-fiction will be in this area of private reading, but there is a place for it in the classroom as well. Many non-fiction books lend themselves to the selection of short, self-contained units for classroom presentation. Sometimes these extracts will be used for their intrinsic value and nothing more: books like *An Orkney Tapestry* by George Mackay Brown and *The Silver Bough* by F. Marian McNeill can yield some very interesting and palatable material on Scottish customs and folklore, but these are not books that we would expect most pupils to tackle and enjoy on their own. Sometimes, however, extracts of this kind can be used to stimulate an interest in the parent work and the area of interest or activity with which it deals. Extracts from books like John Prebble's *Culloden*, George MacDonald Fraser's *The Steel Bonnets*, Donald Caskie's *The Tartan Pimpernel*, Fraser Darling's *Island Years* and David Stephen's *Highland Animals* could serve such a purpose.

There are, of course, non-fiction books which a teacher might wish to deal with in their entirety in class. Some of the ones we have mentioned could fall into this category (*Culloden* and *The Tartan Pimpernel* for example). They will tend to be books with a strong human interest, perhaps with a strong biographical or autobiographical element, books like Gavin Maxwell's *The House of Elrig*, Cliff Hanley's *Dancing in the Streets*, Molly Weir's *Shoes Were for Sunday*, Evelyn Cowan's *Spring Remembered* or Ian Niall's *A Galloway Childhood*. It should be borne in mind, too, that in fourth year and even in fifth year, there is considerable scope for the use of more ephemeral material from magazines like *The Scots Magazine* and from newspapers (e.g. *The Scotsman's* weekend supplement).

The number of major prose or dramatic works that can be studied in class is obviously limited and teachers may feel that there are fewer Scottish plays than novels which merit inclusion in a literature programme at this stage. This is certainly true of fifth year. Perhaps only Bridie has a strong claim, and *The Anatomist* might be the play most likely to be popular and successful with the pupils. There is, too, an excellent play on a Scottish subject by an English dramatist, namely John Arden's *Armstrong's Last Goodnight* which could be read in conjunction with some of the Border Ballads and parts of Fraser's *The Steel Bonnets*. Robert McLellan's *Jamie the Saxt* lends itself to a similar treatment. Other plays which might be considered—like Lindsay's *A Satire of the Three Estates*, Bill Bryden's *Willie Rough* and Roddy McMillan's *The Bevellers*—all have in their different ways problems which might make teachers reluctant to use them as class texts. There might still be a place for such plays, however. A video tape is available of a performance of *The Three Estates** and there is at present something of a renaissance in the Scottish theatre: plays like Bryden's *Benny Lynch*, Hector MacMillan's *The Rising*, Stewart Conn's *I Didn't Always Live Here* and John McGrath's *The Cheviot, the Stag and the Black, Black Oil* have all had considerable success in the theatre and, in some cases, on television. Some senior pupils at least might derive considerable benefit from theatre visits and a judicious use of the television set.

The situation with regard to fourth year is less straightforward. There is still a place at this level for the short play. There are, in fact, a number of good, entertaining Scottish one-act plays which make no pretensions to being great literature but which could be read with profit and enjoyment at this stage. Unfortunately many of these plays are out of print. Millar and Low's *Five Scottish One-Act Plays* contains plays like Bridie's 'The Pardoner's Tale' and Corrie's 'Hewers of Coal' but plays like Alexander Reid's 'The Lass Wi the Muckle Mou' and 'The Warld's Wonder' or the plays of James Scotland (e.g. 'The Daurk Assize') are not available in editions suitable for school use. We have argued the importance and usefulness of drama in the section on the older non-academic pupil. Both the need and the material to satisfy the need exist. We would hope that some publishers might take steps to make that material available.

We have already suggested in this section the use of records, films, television and live theatre performances. It is worth mentioning that some very valuable work has been done recently and will, we hope, continue to be done by B.B.C. Schools Scotland. Their radio programme *Scottish Writing* has produced some very interesting material thematically arranged and has dealt critically but constructively with certain authors and with individual texts.

Both in this section and elsewhere we have stressed the importance of studying Scottish literature in the larger context of English and World literature. It is worth mentioning that at fourth year level there exists the opportunity of studying it in the context of Scottish history. An opportunity for co-operation between English and History departments is offered by the optional nominated topic 'Changing Life in Scotland (1760–1820)' in Ordinary Grade Alternative History the syllabus for which specifies 'some knowledge of the literature, learning, architecture, art and music of the period—especially where first-hand treatment is possible—and of the personal contributions of e.g. Robert Burns and Walter Scott'.

*See Films and Videotapes (p. 105).

# The General Sixth

In most schools, pupils who have already gained an S.C.E. Higher pass and are under-taking no further certificate work in English are expected to take in Year VI some form of 'post-Higher' course involving English studies. This may be a traditional English subject course or some kind of general or liberal studies programme in which English naturally plays a part; but whatever form it takes, it generally labours under certain limitations. The most serious of these is shortage of time: we would suppose that in most schools not more than two periods per week are available. This dis-advantage is compounded by the fact that the personnel of the class frequently varies from period to period. Not surprisingly General English enjoys a relatively low priority when set beside pupils' certificate subjects and as a result pupil motivation is rather low.

It is only realistic to identify these constraints as defining features of any non-specialist English course in Year VI. At the same time we recognise that the situation contains its own compensating opportunities and advantages. Freed as the group is from examination pressures, at least within the subject, the teacher has the chance to be flexible and range widely. He may assume a certain level of competence and maturity in his pupils and usually enjoys the benefits associated with smallness of class size. Bearing these considerations in mind we believe that, in its content, a Sixth Year General English Syllabus might well consist of a wide variety of short units of work and in its method exploit discussion techniques as fully as possible. Such a course is likely to be fragmentary, but it can also be fruitfully opportunist.

Traditionally, English teachers have valued the Sixth Year general periods, how-ever few and ragged they may have been, for the chance they have given to range widely—often in fitful pursuit of the individual teacher's or pupil's enthusiasms—into current affairs, psychology, philosophy, religion, politics, and into the sciences and the other arts. This is as it should be. Certainly we do not think it likely or even desirable that a systematic course on Scottish Literature be offered in this class. We do think it profitable, however, to introduce Scottish elements into any such course.

Scottish literature with its wealth of lyric poetry and short stories is well able to supply material for short self-contained study units, one to three periods in length, of the type that we consider appropriate to the Sixth Year General Syllabus.

These units may consist of:

(a) single works, e.g.:

The Tale of the Wolf, The Fox and the Cadger (Henryson)
The Praise of Ben Dorain (trans. from Gaelic of Duncan Ban Macintyre by Crichton Smith, Akros)
The Holy Fair (Burns)
Docken afore his Peers (Murray)—*Penguin Book of Scottish Verse*
Centre of Centres (MacCaig)—*Penguin Modern Poets 21*
The Two Drovers (Scott)
Thrawn Janet (Stevenson)
The Outgoing of the Tide (Buchan)—*Scottish Short Stories* ed. Urquhart
Smeddum (Grassic Gibbon)—*Scottish Short Stories* ed. Urquhart
The Seller of Silk Shirts (Mackay Brown)—*A Calendar of Love*

(b) invidual authors, e.g.:

Fred Urquhart
Ian H. Finlay
Dorothy K. Haynes
J. C. Milne
William Soutar
Edwin Morgan

(c) *types* of material, e.g.: ballads, folk songs, bothy ballads, 'concrete' poems, short stories, one-acters, monologues.

(d) *pairings* of Scottish and non-Scottish texts and authors, e.g.:

Chaucer's 'Pardoner's Tale' and Bridie's 'Pardoner's Tale'
the animal poems of Norman MacCaig and Ted Hughes
the 'peasant' poems of Ian Crichton Smith, R. S. Thomas and Seamus Heaney
Scottish and English war poetry
Scottish and Irish stories
Bothy ballads and American work songs
*The Anatomist* (Bridie) and *An Enemy of the People* (Ibsen)
*Willie Rough* (Bryden) and *Close the Coal House Door* (Plater)
*The Taste of too Much* (Hanley) and *Catcher in the Rye* (Salinger)
*Remedy is None* (McIlvanney) and *Hamlet*
Grassic Gibbon and Steinbeck

(e) *pairings* of traditional and contemporary Scottish material, e.g.:

Satire in Burns, Garioch and Alexander Scott
To the Merchants of Edinburgh (Dunbar) and The Sparrows in George Square (Morgan)
Traditional ballads and their modern interpretations—The Baron of Brackley and Letter from the Countess (D. N. Black)—*Scottish Short Stories 1973*
The Silkie of Sule Skerry and Sealskin Trousers (Linklater)
Kind Kittock and Kind Kitty (Linklater)
The Lads of Wamphray, The Death of Parcy Reed, Johnnie Armstrong and *Armstrongs's Last Goodnight* (Arden)

(f) short thematic groupings—Scottish topics, e.g.:

*The Forty-Five*
*A History of Scotland*—Rosalind Mitchison (pp. 337–343)
Culloden and After—Crichton Smith

Masque of Princes—Mackay Brown
Battlefield near Inverness—MacCaig
A Near-sichtit Whig View—Garioch
Culloden—Mackay Brown
universal themes illustrated by Scottish material, e.g.:

*Growing up*

Novels: *Morning Tide*—Gunn
        *The Last Summer*—Crichton Smith
        *The Taste of too Much*—Hanley

Autobiography:
Edwin Muir's Autobiography, Chapter 3
Growing up in the West—McIlvanney
(in *Memoirs of a Modern Scotland*, edited Karl Miller)

The thematic possibilities are boundless but we draw particular attention, in the Scottish context, to

  (i) the sense of *local* identity, both at national and local levels, e.g.:
*Edinburgh,* a grouping of poems
To the Merchants of Edinburgh (Dunbar)
Elegy on Lucky Wood (Ramsay)
The Daft Days (Fergusson)
Marmion, canto IV (Scott)
Caller Herrin' (Lady Nairne)
Ille Terrarum (Stevenson)
Old Wife in High Spirits (MacDiarmid)
I was born in this City (Ruthven Todd)
Under the Eildon Tree (Goodsir Smith)
Old Edinburgh (MacCaig)
Jean Brodie's Children (Crichton Smith)
Haar in Princes Street (Scott, Alex)
This wifie (Jackson)
A Moral Tale (Bold)

alternatively *Edinburgh* in the poems of Robert Garioch, e.g.:

Embro to the Ploy
Garioch's Repone
At Robert Fergusson's Grave
Did Ye See Me?
I'm Neutral
The Percipient Swan
And they were Richt
Elegy

  (ii) the *language* situation in Scotland, e.g.:
a grouping of short stories
Baubie Huie's Bastard Geet (William Alexander)—*Scottish Short Stories 1800–1900*
Hurricane Jack's Luck-Bird (Neil Munro)—*Para Handy Tales*
The Mennans (Robert MacLellan)—*Scottish Short Stories*, Urquhart
The Rain Dance (Alan Spence)—*Scottish Short Stories 1973*
The Story of Jorkel Hayforks (George Mackay Brown)—*A Calendar of Love*
Playing Truant (David Toulmin)—*Hard Shining Corn*

three ghost stories in *Tocher*, Vol. 8:

| | |
|---|---|
| The Child's Skeleton | Lizzie & Andrew Stewart, Perthshire |
| Macphail of Uisinnes | from Gaelic of Duncan MacDonald |
| Dr Driver and the Ghost | Shetland dialect of Brucie Henderson |

Certain Scottish authors have traditionally been or have recently become popular in fifth and earlier years. We believe it worthwhile to build on this earlier work by study of less familiar texts by such authors, e.g.: Burns, Stevenson, Grassic Gibbon, Morgan, the ballads.

We recommend the use of 'non-literary' Scottish material as an element in these short units—particularly contemporary journalism.

We appreciate that the amount of written work undertaken in a general course is likely to be limited. Nevertheless the methods in use in C.S.Y.S. should be borne in mind: many pupils in the general course are of C.S.Y.S. level. In particular we recommend the individual inquiry embodying the same principles as the C.S.Y.S. Dissertation, although less ambitious in scope, as an invaluable method of encouraging pupils to explore Scottish literature. It is highly desirable moreover that the texts read should be exploited as stimuli and models for the pupils' own creative efforts.

It is unlikely that much close literary study in class of longer works such as novels will be tackled in a general course. The most appropriate way in which Scottish fiction can be introduced is by ensuring that the school library carries a good selection of Scottish works for individual reading. We are in favour of the establishment, through the combined resources of Library and English Department, of a 'kit' of Scottish materials suitable for Sixth Year General use.

Opportunities to see drama in performance should be fully exploited. Relatively few schools in Scotland are so remote that they cannot send a bus party, particularly of senior pupils, to a theatre once or twice a year; or avail themselves of the visit of a touring company. The recent appearance of a concerned, entertaining, documentary drama in Scotland has provided schools with attractive opportunities.

Recent Scottish contributions to radio and television drama have been by no means negligible and should be considered whenever possible.

As with C.S.Y.S. we urge the fullest use of the help offered by such agencies as the BBC and the Scottish Arts Council. The relative flexibility possible in a general course should facilitate this. Similarly we believe that opportunities exist for the engineering of links with the other arts in Scotland—music, painting, architecture.

At present, it is true, we can sometimes introduce Scottish literature in Year VI on the strength of its novelty value—something of whose existence the pupils have had no previous idea. It comes as a revelation! This is valuable, as the BBC's excellent schools' broadcasts for senior pupils have shown, but the profit is limited and short-term. Ultimately in having recourse to such a technique we are condemning ourselves. We believe that pupils should not be so deprived that they come with the freshness of total ignorance to Scottish texts in sixth year. Scottish literature should be an essential ingredient of their diet throughout primary and secondary education.

# The Certificate of Sixth Year Studies

Desiderata for courses leading to the award of the Certificate of Sixth Year Studies in English are outlined in the Examination Board's annual syllabus. These give considerable scope for the study of Scottish texts. Perhaps the extent of the opportunity, particularly as regards Paper III, has not been generally realised.

## Dissertation

The criteria for the selection of Scottish material for Dissertation study are, of course, the same as for any other texts: they should be of interest to the pupil, and they should, in the judgement of the teacher, be likely to reward the effort that the pupil is required to expend upon them. With these considerations in mind, we must acknowledge that Scottish texts face strong competition from the whole range of world literature. If our pupils in the end prefer Tolstoy and Mann to Gibbon and Gunn we can have no grounds for disappointment; but we do have some obligation to ensure that they are at least aware of the possibilities of Gibbon and Gunn. We do the cause of our literature no good by thrusting it uncritically upon our pupils. The best we can do is to ensure, enthusiastically, that it gets a fair chance.

Assuming the intrinsic interest and worth of individual texts and authors, we may well think that Scottish works merit consideration as Dissertation material for the following additional reasons:

1. they can appeal to immediate *local* interests.

   (a) Certain writers have a powerful sense of place—Mackay Brown, Gibbon, Gunn, George Blake.

   (b) Groupings of texts permit exploration of local topics—fishing, farming, heavy industry, Glasgow, Edinburgh, Aberdeen.

   (c) Certain texts allow study of local dialect elements—Burns, 'Johnny Gibb', recent Glasgow verse.

2. they offer unusually good opportunities for the study of certain themes, themes which involve what might be regarded as characteristically Scottish preoccupations: the patriarchal family, religious fanaticism, the clash of cultures, getting on, the various dimensions of the 'antisyzygy'.

3. similarly they are exceptionally useful for the study of certain literary types—the ballad, the historical novel.

4. they are virtually the *only* imaginative sources for the study of one theme likely to be of some interest to Scottish pupils—the national identity, 'Scottishness'.

5. they allow for linkage with the other aspects of Scottish life and culture that may be studied in Sixth Year—History, Music, Art, Gaelic, Economics.

6. they allow comparisons and contrasts with the literature of other countries—Scott and Fenimore Cooper, Gibbon and Steinbeck.

The selection of Scottish texts and topics for the C.S.Y.S. Dissertation may seem to be beset with temptations—excessively ambitious, sophisticated themes, distorted non-literary emphases, choice of trivial material—but experience shows that these are dangers common to most Dissertation choices whether Scottish or not. They do not amount to a reason for avoiding Scottish material. As candidates have already demonstrated there is scope here for genuinely original work.

Whilst the 'out-of-print' problem does affect Scottish Dissertation studies it is not such a serious inconvenience at this level since generally only one copy of a work is required. Many local libraries are extremely well placed to support schools in their quest for Scottish texts. Nowhere is the co-operation of the school with the public library likely to prove more fruitful. For suggestions for Scottish language topics see A. J. Aitken's essay.

*Paper I: Creative Writing*

Section A of Paper I implies some study and practice in a variety of literary forms—verse, dialogue, short story, interior monologue, character sketch, discursive essay. It seems only sensible to make use of contemporary Scottish material as models and stimuli for such writing.

In this the teacher has recently had encouraging support from a variety of agencies. It is to be hoped that schools by their response will allow these to continue.

The B.B.C. has since Autumn 1971 provided a valuable radio series *Scottish Writing* which can be harnessed to motivate pupils' own efforts. The Scottish Arts Council's scheme, Writers in Schools, allows pupils to come into lively contact with distinguished contemporary writers. A range of publications such as *Roses and Thorns*, (David Angus, Club Leabhar), *The Fifth Estate* (Aberdeen College of Education), *Setting Out* (eds. Inglis, Martin & Rocheford, Triangle Press, 1972) and the Examination Board's own *Young Scots Writing* has provided challenging samples of the work of senior pupils as students. Finally, *Akros, Lines Review, Scotia Review*, the *Glasgow Review, The Scotsman* and the *Glasgow Herald* and certain B.B.C. Radio 4 Scottish programmes have afforded schools access to the best current Scottish work in progress.

All of these can help to generate the sense of a local cultural 'scene' so important if the pupil is not to feel that he is merely writing school exercises in practice for examinations. As the B.B.C. pamphlet accompanying the first series of *Scottish Writing* puts it,

'We hope the series will make it plain to pupils that there have been and still are many writers in Scotland who have something significant to say about the issues and problems which confront us today, and that their response to these matters is perhaps specially relevant in that they share with the pupils something of the same social and cultural background.'

Part B of Paper I requires training in the writing of well-informed carefully organised, discussion essays. The areas of study regularly appearing in past papers include: religion, education, psychology, social, political and moral issues, history, science, the arts, the environment, the history of ideas. Clearly it would be pointless to attempt to construct a purely Scottish course of reading for any of these topics. Such a course, if it could be produced at all, would be esoteric and limited. What the examination seems to encourage is the study and discussion of two or three concise authoritative modern popularisations dealing with the chosen topic. At this level 'Scottishness' is irrelevant.

Certainly in some of these accounts Scottish figures will have an honourable place— Knox, Hume, Adam Smith, Clerk Maxwell, Raeburn, the Adam brothers, Black, Cullen, Napier, Scott, Hugh Miller, Kelvin, Telford, Watt—but only a place.

Perhaps the only effective way of giving a Scottish dimension to the work which Part B seeks to stimulate is to ensure that pupils are led, wherever appropriate, to relate topics to a Scottish context, in terms of their own present lives. The examiners, after all, clearly hope that pupils will see their chosen topics as matters of immediate interest to themselves. Regular critical consideration of current issues, local, national and international, as they are presented in Scottish press, radio and television is one way of securing such a vital Scottish orientation.

## Paper II: Literature

The literature paper has offered opportunity for the detailed study of the works of several major Scottish authors. To date, Henryson, Scott, MacDiarmid and Grassic Gibbon have appeared. Arguably these are the only ones who can stand comparison with the non-Scottish writers on the syllabus: but it is reasonable to assume that in future others may secure a place—Dunbar, Burns, Hogg, Galt, Stevenson, Bridie, Gunn, MacCaig, Crichton Smith, Mackay Brown.

However, so long as the Paper retains its present form, room for manoeuvre is limited: each Scottish author specified or recommended must be able to offer, in quality and quantity, a challenge similar to that of the non-Scots on the list. Moreover his works must be in print in a reasonably cheap form for school use.

On the positive side, it is surely no bad thing that at Sixth Year level, Scottish writers should be juxtaposed, in the way that Paper II ensures, with the masters of English, European and American literature. It is interesting to note that, so far, candidates have shown relatively little interest in the Scottish authors on the syllabus.

Any course of study engendered by Paper II calls for close reading and discussion of texts and thoughtful personal engagement with them. Awareness of the critical considerations raised by the texts and knowledge of the author's milieu are important but subsidiary. Opportunity for writing on the texts needs to be given.

Such a course is a demanding one and it may well be that for the average post-Higher candidate an attractive alternative approach to Scottish literature may be through Practical Criticism.

## Paper III: Practical Criticism

Paper III affords ample opportunity for the use of Scottish material. If it is taken in conjunction with Paper I, it allows the teacher to devise his own literature syllabus with two guiding principles in mind: that the works chosen should stimulate and provide models for creative writing, and that they should develop the powers of discrimination called for in Practical Criticism.

The only content requirements imposed are that there should be modern poetry, that there should be varieties of prose which permit comparison and contrast, and that there should be some drama.

A syllabus serving both Papers I and III might well contain a wide range of shortish poems. The prose would certainly take in short stories as well as novels and samples of such non-fiction as autobiography, travel writing, historical writing and journalism. Drama might include one-acters. The emphasis of the course would be largely but not exclusively modern.

Scottish writing is obviously well able to supply a substantial proportion of the texts for such a course, particularly since the stress upon comparison allows the fruitful juxtaposition of Scottish and non-Scottish material.

The Scots Language and the Teaching of English in Scotland

# Two Essays

Two topics lying just outside the remit of the sub-committee seemed too important to ignore. These were the Scots Language and the Gaelic Literary Tradition. What follows are statements on these topics by two authorities. They are personal statements and do not necessarily reflect the views of the S.C.C.E.; but the S.C.C.E. is pleased to be able to offer them as contributions to the discussion and understanding of areas of knowledge too little explored by Scots teachers of English.

# The Scots Language and the Teacher of English in Scotland

A. J. Aitken

### The state of Scots today

This writer's favoured model of the Scottish language today represents it as a con-flation or merger of two closely related languages or dialects known respectively as 'Scots' and 'English' which had previously led fairly separate existences. Since the 17th and 18th centuries, when the merger chiefly occurred, the conflated language has offered to speakers and writers of Scots a very large number of stylistic choices between distinctively Scottish expressions and their general English equivalents: in word-forms and words like, say, *hame* and *darg* versus *home* and *job of work* as well as in a few grammatical constructions like *every time I sees him I aye thinks that* and its 'standard' equivalent. Though the particular choices at the disposal of particular individuals vary according to region, social class, personal linguistic receptivity and various other factors, so that certain people dispose of many more than do others, some choices at least are available to all. By selecting differently from these, Scottish people can—and do—arrive at an almost infinite number of different spoken styles, varying from occasion to occasion and individual to individual. In practice the vari-ation is somewhat less than it might otherwise be because of the tendency in th e system towards stylistic polarisation, a tendency displayed in some regions and individuals more markedly than in others: between the stylistic pole, traditionally regarded as appropriate to public or formal and middle-class speech, where the Scottish options are largely disallowed, and the opposite one where a greater or lesser use of Scottish options is acceptable.

As well as options such as these, which can be thought of as occupying the poles, this conflated system also contains a large body of material common to all styles, including both the most fully Scots and the most fully English: this may be thought of as the central area or 'core' of the system. This 'common core' material includes those phonological, grammatical and lexical elements which had long been shared by the two component dialects: words like *bed, table, fine, winter, get, keep,* virtually the entire grammatical system, such as nearly all the uses of the *–s* inflection, with only a few exceptions like that cited above, and the *system* of sounds, both the underlying one and its surface manifestation as 'accent'. Indeed it is only these fundamental shared elements which have made possible the merger of the two dialects concerned.

Innovations in the grammatical system of world English and, still more obviously, the profusion of new loan-words, compounds, coinages and new uses of established words which are constantly enriching our vocabulary, supply further additions to the 'common core': expressions like *chauffeur, chain store, macaroni, spaghetti, wireless, phone, taxi, anorak, karate, zombie, up the creek* and *O.K.* For these new resources are of course just as much at the disposal of 'dialect speakers' as of 'speakers of standard English'.

This is only one way in which those elements in the system which are not distinctively Scottish have come more and more to dominate it—in which it is gradually becoming less Scottish. Another is a now long-standing habit of even those Scots who continue to use both Scottish and relatively un-Scottish styles on different occasions to import forms and usages from their 'public' or 'English' style into their 'private' one. So the older Scottish options the system offers have tended to be chosen less often by fewer people. This process has no doubt been under way since the 17th century when written English and, in speech, an approximation to the spoken 'standard' of upper-class Englishmen was first adopted as the 'public' language of Scotsmen also and the essentials of the present situation established.

In such ways as these, as is regularly claimed in the innumerable aprioristic assertions made by almost everyone who has ever since the 18th century talked or written about the history and condition of Scots, 'Scots' is indeed 'dying'. But these claims are commonly greatly exaggerated. So gradual is the 'decline' that all of the statements made in this part of this essay about current Scots could be applied with equal validity to the state of affairs in the 18th century itself. And, despite all that has been said, the number of distinctive Scottish expressions which continue in daily currency remains astonishingly large—as a glance at some of the *Scottish National Dictionary's* 30,000 or so entries, few of which are noted in the dictionary as wholly obsolete, will remind us. According to a recent estimate of the present writer's for a desk dictionary of English, most middle-class, English-speaking Scots retain at their active disposal as overt or covert Scotticisms at the very least several hundred native words or turns of phrase (such as *ceilidh, chuckie-stane,* (a good) *conceit* (of oneself), *couthy, curfuffle*) and retain a passive knowledge of many more, along with a host of Scottish word-*forms* (like *hieland* and *hame*).

It is fair, then, to say that in Scottish speech, at the 'dialect' level which we have so far only considered, the 'common core' and imported 'English' element is dominant and the native Scots one, large as this still is, recessive. In many ways this is less true at the level of 'accent', those rather minute (but audible and highly 'indexical') differences in the precise realisations as utterance which different regional and social groups give to 'the same sounds'—the different ways that different speakers have, for example, of pronouncing 'the sound *r*'—and similarly distributed differences in habits of intonation, relative stress, tempo and general posture of the speech organs. Most of the features of the accents of most native-educated Lowland Scots derive from the earlier Scottish history of native Scottish speech. The characteristic Scottish contrasts between pairs like *brood* and *brewed*, and *greed* and *agreed*, and *tide* and *tied*, for example, return to an all but exclusively Scottish sound-change which can be dated quite certainly to the 17th century or earlier, before Scottish speech was much affected by southern English at all. Not that by any means all the Scottish accents remain entirely unanglicised. Those which remain most completely native are the rural and urban working-class accents, whereas in the typical accent of the white-collar classes in Scotland (including most of its school-teachers) a few English-derived features have superseded native ones, thus supplying a social differential.

But it seems still to be true that the accents of most Scots today lie within the range delimited by the two types just alluded to—from the fully localised and Scottish working-class accents to the less localised but still mainly Scottish accents of many middle-class Scots. The accent of the laird class, on the other hand, is of a very different type, and, unlike these, has no roots in Scotland at all: it is simply the same high-status accent of English origin which is obligatory in 'county' circles in both England and Scotland. But because it is associated with socially influential and prestigious individuals—it is perhaps the only accent used in Scotland which carries positive cachet, and we have also, unhappily, allowed it to dominate the broadcasting media—it is admired for its 'elegance' and consequently is tending to pull the whole system in an 'English' direction. One result is a number of 'hybrid' accents heard from some middle-class Scots—those which retain some of the usual Scots features but have abandoned others such as the 'post-vocalic r' in words like *third* or *form*. A different sort of hybrid is the 'Kelvinside' or 'Morningside' variety (known as a stereotype since the last century) with its several 'hyper-correct' vowel qualities.

Now in some ways the set-up just described as it exists to day is not all that unique to Scots. In other regions of the English-speaking world and, of course, in other languages, the local vernaculars and a less localised spoken variety of the 'standard language' are interlinked in similar bipolar systems offering a range of choices of style. In these other regions the more and less conscious and controlled 'shifts' or 'drifts' from one dialectal style to another in response to changes in the formality of the situation also occur just as they do among Scots speakers. There too one meets speakers who make permanent adjustments of their stylistic base, most often in adolescence and early adulthood, from one area of the overall range of dialect styles and accents to another, in response to the demands of 'social mobility'. As a set of regional dialects, Scots constitutes a northern extension of the general English dialect continuum, so that many features often thought of as characteristically Scottish in fact occur in English dialect speech as far as 100 or more miles south of the Border— for example, forms like *hame* or *sair* or *hoose* (albeit slightly differently pronounced) or words like *kirk* or *lass* or *bairn*.

But in other ways the Scottish situation *is* special. Though it is true that a proportion of the dialect features often taken as typically Scots are not bounded by the Border, many others are (such as the highly characteristic *tide* and *tied* contrast), and the Scottish dialects have their own extremely fine network of differences, peculiar to themselves, as befits a language settled in its present locations for over 700 years. In no other English-speaking region are the native or vernacular options so numerous, so striking and so institutionalised. Scots has more, and more striking, formal contrasts between sets of cognates like *hame* and *home*, *sair* and *sore*, and so on, than other comparable dialects. If many of the more frequently used and 'basic' items of vocabulary are 'common core' items, many others, including some of the commonest, are variables belonging to the optional parts of the system. So the stylistic contrasts that Scots speech offers are more obtrusive and more pervasive than in anything comparable in other regions.

In some parts of Scotland, such as Buchan and Shetland, some speakers display a form of 'style-switching' that could fairly be called 'dialect-switching'; that is, they can move, for example when turning from neighbours to strangers, as may happen in a local shop, from a fairly full local Doric to a fairly 'pure' standard English (spoken in the local accent, of course). The presence of dialect-switching virtuosi of this sort is rather special to Scotland in the English-speaking world and was no doubt once much more general here. Admittedly, what most speakers in most areas now practise is a far less controlled and more inconsistent or fluctuating kind of 'style-drifting', which resembles the similar sort of thing met furth of Scotland. But even with these speakers, the distances between their opposed stylistic poles are often markedly greater than occur elsewhere.

Only in Scotland has style-switching in this obtrusive way been institutionalised as a regular and characteristic and indeed predominant part of the technique of poetry of most genres since as far back as the Middle Scots period. Since the stylistic contrasts play such a noticeable part in Scottish social behaviour they have from the outset dominated the dialogue and sometimes the narrative of Scottish fiction in a range of subtly differentiated types to an extent unparalleled in any other 'regional' literature in English.

In the face of so much that is special about the Scottish language, it is astonishing that its condition and situation receive so little attention in our institutions of education.

### Free speech in the Scottish classroom

In Scotland, as elsewhere, social evaluations of others based on their speech usually masquerade as judgements of the speech itself. In reality these are inferences from certain 'indexical' linguistic features of speech about the social background and educational history or alternatively—but often unjustly—social pretensions of the speaker. In the scale of approval or denigration which these evaluations make up, ranging from 'fine', 'clear', 'beautiful', 'attractive', through 'rich', 'vigorous', 'homely' on the one hand, and 'lah-de-dah' and 'high-falutin' on the other, the varieties which come off worst are the 'uncouth', 'ugly', 'sloppy' or 'slovenly' speech of the urban working-classes. The features most often singled out for the condemnation of the latter varieties are certain accent-features—the 'post-vocalic glottal stop', certain vowel qualities, and certain rhythm and intonation features. As it happens, the only one of these features which is at all an innovation (in common with other British urban speech) is the 'glottal stop'; the rest are fully native, and so can claim a rather more ancient 'lineage' than their innovative, partly anglicised, middle-class equivalents. In the company of such accent-features certain Scots dialect forms and usages— the stigmatised pronunciations of *nothing* and *catholic*, other Scots dialect forms like *hame* or *hoose*, the interrogative tags *eh?* or *eh-no?*, the free use of the pause-filler *ken?*, and grammatical rules slightly different from those of English, such as *I never shoulda went*—all these too are subject to stigma. It is true that there are welcome signs that some of our young people care far less about conformity in such things (in themselves and others) than their elders did and do. Nevertheless judgements of this kind continue to play their part in maintaining social differentials to the disadvantage of working-class speakers, including working-class children. As teachers we have a duty to our pupils—and to truth—to combat such superstitions and by no means help to perpetuate them.

As things are, a schoolchild's first confrontation with the arbitrary values which society places on small differences in speech very often comes in school itself. Here he meets a teacher with a rather different style of speaking and evidently relying on a stereotype of what is estimable in speech which excludes the speech of the child himself. Now it may be important for the pupil that he should learn at some stage about how the establishment values his and others' speech. So it might be argued that those teachers who are given to correcting 'errors' in their pupils' speech and so providing forcible reminders of these values are doing their pupils a necessary service. Against this machiavellian argument, some linguists respond that this kind of treatment is likely to be harmful to the child. For, they claim, by producing divided loyalties about his native speech, with its powerful connotations of family and friends, and by inducing the habit of self-monitoring for linguistic 'errors', it instils uncertainty and self-consciousness. So the pupil is made tongue-tied in *any* form of language. The fundamental objection against this practice, however, is its implied arrogance— however 'enlightened' the teacher's motives seem to be.

This does not mean that children should be permanently shielded from the knowledge that some forms of speech are apt to induce unfavourable responses in others, perhaps including potential employers, simply by being different. Some children will of course adjust to this realisation as part of their normal linguistic development on the evidence that society in general—other speakers, the media—will provide. But others will in adolescence only be beginning to do so. There may even be some who are destined to remain largely unaware of this throughout their lives except in the crudest ways.

In a recent study of some aspects of the speech of Glasgow and its educational implications it is claimed that children are entitled to be informed objectively of the standards in this respect by which they may be judged when they leave school, and that a confrontation with this unpleasant fact of society should not be allowed to go by default. But this is only possible in the secondary school when the child has sufficient personal maturity and linguistic sophistication to tackle such questions. Some of the discussion sessions on language which are suggested below might be one way in which the relevant matters could be brought into the open. What consequent action, if any, each pupil chooses is his private affair.

It may be argued that reading (and acting and reciting) and writing standard English will suffer if we substitute a permissive régime in matters of dialect and accent for an insistence that all speaking which takes place in the classroom be in 'correct English'. And certainly most reading and writing in Scottish schools must continue to be in the principal 'public' language, English. But on scrutiny this argument turns out to have little to do with command of vocabulary and sentence-manipulation, since these involve skills which are independent of dialect or accent. As speakers like Jimmy Reid or some of the characters in Bryden's *Willie Rough* attest, it is just as possible to speak copiously, fluently and effectively in a Glasgow accent or a Paisley dialect as in Oxford English. What this argument is really about is the possibility that some dialect pronunciations and a trifling number of deviant grammatical usages may occasion a few 'errors' in English spelling and grammar. But even if it were true that the only way of securing conformity here were by insistence on conformity to something like establishment speech, it ought to be questioned whether this can conceivably repay the potential price in loss of confidence and fluency.

So long as our society continues to insist on 'correct' spelling and 'grammatical' speech as a hall-mark of 'educated' status, it is right that pupils who need and want these accomplishments should be helped to realise them. And all members of the class should from time to time have the chance to perform in suitable roles or situations in the public forms of speech and in this way to learn to move about or across the whole range of Scottish speech-styles. But this is not the same as saying that we should rigidly insist on one 'standard' of classroom speech on all occasions or that we ought to impose the various kinds of 'correctness' involved indiscriminately on all our pupils. Psychologists, educationists and linguists are now pleading for far more talk in classrooms everywhere, and especially in Scotland with its tradition of 'receptive' education. Their aims of encouraging self-confidence and fluency in speaking will only succeed if this talk is uninhibited by externally imposed standards of 'correctness'.

The free dialogue between dialect-varieties (the teacher's 'English' or 'Scottish English' and the pupil's 'Scots') which this implies is perfectly natural and healthy in our linguistic situation and commonplace in the adult world. If in the course of this occasional difficulties of comprehension present themselves on one side or the other, this could be a welcome opportunity for each party to learn tolerance of and display interest in the other's language.

*Writing and Reading Scots*

The 'common core' element is not the whole of the vocabulary and usage of the Scots language, and formal and utilitarian registers in 'English' not the only ways in which writing can be practised. Scottish pupils ought not to be deprived of the chance of exploring the range of Scots styles, so becoming players as well as spectators in their own literature.

So the invented dialogue and monologue included in role-playing projects and similar exercises should offer opportunities for the observation and manipulation of varieties of *Scots*, along the scale described in the opening section of this essay, as well as of varieties of 'English'. This will happen quite naturally if the majority of these exercises have the kind of local and Scottish settings within which Scottish pupils belong. The problems posed in composing dialogue of these kinds in written form could, for the more senior pupils, initiate important discussions on speech-variety and the relationship of spelling to speech. To write, on other occasions, a story or poem using 'classical' Scots, would pose a different set of problems.

An obvious, and perhaps essential, preparation for writing in these modes would be the reading of literature in which similar problems were tackled. While this might naturally include standard classics such as *The House with the Green Shutters*— a useful model for an attempt at differentiating characters by distinct linguistic features—it could perhaps most helpfully include something in the local form of Scots, even if, as is likely, the text has to be provided as duplicated 'hand-out': a list of possible sources is provided in the bibliography to the booklet *Lowland Scots* mentioned below, but the teacher's own reading may suggest more adventurous and more recent examples. From some of this, the pupils can be shown that spelling can be simultaneously conventional and variable (as with 'classical' Scots spelling) and also how it is possible, within limits, to depart from the conventions in the direction of greater phonetic precision or simply for novelty, for realist or comic effect. They might then find it fun to experiment in similar techniques for themselves.

*Talking and writing about Scots speech*

Any writing or reading in Scots which a class does is likely to provoke questions such as: why in this form and not in 'ordinary' English? is the Scots true-to-life or should it be? There are other topics in this area, also of obvious social and political relevance. Some of these have already been mentioned in this essay. Others include: if there are different sorts of Scots, is there any ground for valuing one kind more highly than another? What are or should be the respective places for Scots and English in our society? is the treatment by the media of different sorts of Scots adequate and fair?

Whatever linguistic sophistication the teacher himself can contribute to these discussions will clearly be valuable. If possible, it should take in some acquaintance with the elements of phonetics and with sociolinguistic principles, as these are set out in the works mentioned below. But it does not call for advanced knowledge of the latest refinements of modern linguistics. What it should include is as much knowledge as the teacher can muster of contemporary Scots speech, particularly the local variety, so that he will know what are the different linguistic standards or rules involved in the whole situation.

A further dimension can be given to discoveries by the pupils about the current situation if the teacher can also tell them something of the history of Scots. He should aim to explain how it and other varieties, especially standard English, have come to differ and how their own situation has come about. This could well arise from the study of the earlier native literature, with its display of change over the centuries. In discussing this historical development the teacher may also wish to raise the issue of the place of Gaelic in past and present-day Scotland. One manifestation of this which lies conveniently to the hand of all school-teachers throughout Scotland is the local place-names.

The local speech is an obvious—and, if the arguments advanced so far have any validity, obviously fruitful—subject for group work and for Certificate of Sixth Year Studies dissertations, as the C.S.Y.S. handbook itself recognises. There is not space here to do more than hint at some of the possibilities. For one of these the class might compile a list of 100 or so native words and meanings (one way would be to consult glossaries to local dialect writings) which were in potential use in the local speech. Each pupil might then investigate by simple direct questioning the extent to which each item was actually used by, merely passively known to or wholly unknown to several informants representing different generations, and the global results of this assembled, discussed and reported on.

There is in the Scottish situation no shortage of the kind of linguistic variables usable in sociolinguistic investigation and at the same time comparatively easily and more often than not unambiguously identifiable by untrained hearers: like *-ing* ∼ *-in* the use or non-use of the glottal stop when the option arises, *dinna* ∼ *don't*, and others. Using some of these it ought to be possible for a senior class to conduct a valid sociolinguistic investigation within their own school and a neighbouring primary school, perhaps with a total of 24 informants, 8 of these from among themselves, the others from two younger classes. The investigation would employ the principles and techniques of similar pieces of professional research, though with a shorter interview time and using traditional Scots spelling in place of phonetic script. The results of this, derived from transcriptions (in spelling) of tape-recorded interviews would then be correlated in the usual way with the non-linguistic factors of age and sex and any others which obtruded themselves. Certainly the time needed for such an investigation, even with group collaboration, would be substantial (upwards of 24 periods?), but much would be learned from it, on research principles and methods as well as on how and, more speculatively, why people vary in their ways of speaking.

*Some relevant books*

There are many works on English Linguistics with a bias either towards English English or American English. Nothing comparable exists for Scots and Scots English —neither a full-scale history of the language nor a survey of its present condition. But a modest approach to this and the obvious first piece of reading for anyone beginning or renewing his study of Scots, is the booklet *Lowland Scots* (Association for Scottish Literary Studies, Occasional Papers No. 2, 1973, price 75p, obtainable from the Association's Treasurer, Dr D. S. Hewitt, Department of English, University of Aberdeen). This book contains excellent introductory essays on Middle Scots and on modern literary Scots (including something on 'Lallans'); it therefore seemed less important to devote space to these subjects in the present essay. There is no space here to repeat or expand on the bibliography in this work, which supplies many of the needed references to writings on Middle and Modern Scots. More directly focussed on the present situation is *The Scots Language in Education* (Association for Scottish Literary Studies, Occasional Papers No. 3, 1974, obtainable from Dr D. S. Hewitt, as above, price 6op, or from Aberdeen College of Education). Particularly relevant to one of the themes of the present essay is Peter Trudgill's paper in the latter collection, 'Sociolinguistics and Scots dialects', with its excellent brief guide to the literature of sociolinguistics.

An example of the kind of questionnaire which might be used in a sociolinguistic investigation is to be found in P. Trudgill *The Social Differentiation of English in Norwich* (Cambridge University Press, 1974). Unfortunately, good recorded specimens of authentic contemporary spoken Scots of several regions and social varieties are not at present publicly available (though there is a little Scots in *English with a Dialect*, B.B.C. Records, R.E.C. 173). For this purpose the teacher must meantime make do with printed specimens, such as those in W. Grant and J. Main Dixon *Manual of Modern Scots* (Cambridge University Press, 1921).

## Conclusion

None of the suggestions made above are meant to exclude those Scottish pupils who, for whatever reason, are not themselves speakers of 'dialect'. Such people are not of course thereby insulated from the whole local situation and their own speech (which may well retain rather more Scottish features than is usually realised) participates in the total system described in the opening paragraphs of this essay. In any case, since they are Scots, the Scottish tongue is an important part of their environment and their history.

What is important about these suggestions, which may seem presumptuous to some, utopian to others, and, it may be, quite misguided to others again, is their underlying thesis: that our pupils deserve the chance to learn as much as we can offer them about their own language in their own environment, about its history and its present condition and their own position in this, at the same time acquiring tolerance for the language of their fellow-countrymen and some degree of security in speech for themselves. This would seem to call for much more talk and writing of and about Scots in our schools.

# The Gaelic Literary Tradition

John MacInnes

I believe it is still possible in Scotland to leave school without hearing anything, or at least anything of interest, about Gaelic. Those children who hear about the Picts and the Scots, and the rest, are most unlikely to learn that the Scots, quite simply, were the Gaels; that their language, which spread throughout the country, is still a living tongue; and that it has been used by generations of major Scottish writers, some of whom are living at the present time. The importance of Gaelic and its literature as a distinctive element within the greater unit of Scotland needs no stressing, but it may be useful to indicate the extent to which Gaelic impinges upon the rest of Scotland, or at a certain stage of history pervades it. Modern scholarship is becoming aware that even in Lothian, Gaelic settlement began very much earlier and by that token was very much denser than has hitherto been thought. Historical evidence can of course connect with literature in different ways: it must surely add immediacy to the most cursory study of Gaelic if it is realised, for instance, that Gaelic place-names extend down to and even beyond the English border.

The history of the Gaelic people and their language in Scotland covers over six centuries of expansion and development followed by a slightly longer period of slow decline. Gaelic was established in what is now Scotland about the beginning of the 6th century by colonists from Ireland, the older Scotia. By the early part of the 11th century King Duncan—the gentle Duncan of Shakespeare's *Macbeth*—had become ruler of the mainland of modern Scotland. The authority of these early Gaelic Kings over a large portion of their realm was merely nominal: the Hebrides, for instance, and sizable tracts of the North and West were under Norse domination. Nevertheless, the existence of a Gaelic speaking court, with its attendant patronage, was of great importance to Gaelic literature, the exponents of which were organised in what practically amounted to a caste system. When the court became Anglicised under the sons of Malcolm Canmore and Queen Margaret, the setback was profound and permanent. No longer the *sermo regius* of Scotland, Gaelic was now fated never to fulfil what had seemed to be its destiny: to become the language of cultured society throughout the kingdom and the medium of expression in its leading institutions. Instead there began the process which ultimately banished it to the remote and inaccessible parts of the land; and although development did not by any means cease, Gaelic literature became largely cut off from the influence of the great innovating movements of post-mediaeval Europe.

Meanwhile in the lowlands of Scotland the northern English dialect was being developed as the national language. This, and the evolution of a distinctive Scots literature, meant that Scotland became a country of two literary cultures. Down to the 16th century the term 'Scots' was used to describe Gaelic, and what we now call Scots was then called Inglis. Later, Gaelic was frequently referred to as Irish or Erse—different forms of the same word. This change in nomenclature serves to illustrate the shift in cultural orientation which the development of the Lowland tongue produced in Gaelic society. Ireland now reassumes a dominant role; in relation to it Scotland becomes something of a cultural periphery. In that redefined situation the principal focus of Gaelic political and cultural organisation was the confederation known as the Lordship of the Isles. This semi-independent state, which exercised influence, if not always authority, over a considerable part of the North West mainland was not finally destroyed until the mid-16th century and some of its cultural resonances linger in Gaelic tradition to the present day. Partly because of these facts of history we normally associate Gaelic with the north west and tend to forget that it was spoken in Galloway, in the extreme south west, until well on in the 17th century, and possibly later; or that on the east, Aberdeenshire Gaelic died out only a couple of years ago; or, indeed, that only some forty miles from Edinburgh it is still spoken in Perthshire.

The special relationship with Ireland remained intact until the 17th century. In spite of differences, political or religious, Ireland and Gaelic Scotland continued to be one cultural area. As the vernacular dialects of the two countries began to diverge, the mandarin class who cultivated the arts standardised a common language, a flexible, classical form of Gaelic. These learned men moved freely throughout the lands of 'the sea-divided Gael' enjoying a kind of diplomatic immunity. Inevitably they promoted a sense of cultural solidarity, within Scotland as well as between Scotland and Ireland.

In this way Scots Gaelic participates in one of the great literatures of mediaeval Europe. It is essentially an aristocratic tradition, developed from an ancient native stock under the influence of mediaeval European rhetoric. In the Dark Ages, poets of the highest caste specialised in historical and mythological lore. Such a poem is the 'Scottish Lay' composed in the reign of Malcolm Canmore and addressed to the poet's peers, the aristocracy of birth as well as the aristocracy of learning:

'O all ye learned ones of Alba
O stately yellow-haired company'

Later reorganisations, perhaps due to the Anglo-Norman invasions of Ireland and Scotland, modified their role to that of panegyrists who wrote to celebrate great men, wherever patrons who were willing to pay for a poem could be found. They remained a professional intelligentsia, justifying a highly stratified society, advising and exhorting their patrons freely, but also on occasion expressing adverse criticism.

But they did not confine themselves to praise-poetry, nor was all poetry written by professionals. Among the aristocracy there were men and women who were sufficiently conversant with classical Gaelic and skilled enough in the conventions of its court poetry to write subtle, elegant and passionate poems, even if they did not observe the purists' rules of consonantal and vowel rhyme, or all the other ornaments demanded by the poetic schools. Thus we find Isobel, first Countess of Argyll, composing a charming little love-poem in the 15th century:

'There is a youth comes wooing me; oh King of Kings, may he succeed! would he were stretched upon my breast, with his body against my skin.
If every thing were as I wish it, never should we be far divided, though it is all too little to declare, since he does not see how the case is.

It cannot be, till his ship comes home, a thing most pitiful for us both; he in the east and I in the west, so that our desires are not fulfilled.'

In the same manuscript there is an elegy by the widow of the chief of the MacNeills. She addresses the rosary, remembering the hand that had held it until that night. The poem draws upon conventional images of praise, but it is nonetheless poignant and tender.

'Rosary that has roused my tear, dear the finger that was wont to be upon you; dear the heart, hospitable and generous, that owned you ever until tonight . . .
A mouth whose winning speech would wile the hearts of all in every land; lion of white-walled Mull, hawk of Islay of smooth plains . . .
Mary Mother, who did nurse the King, may she guard me on every path, and her Son who created each creature, rosary that has roused my tear.'

When the tradition is nearing its end in the eighteenth century, we find Niall Mór MacMhuirich in South Uuist writing as elegantly as any of his predecessors. His 'Message of the Eyes' is in the same convention as the Countess of Argyll's poem. The great scholar Robin Flower described it succinctly: 'The subject is love, and not the direct passion of the folk-singers or the high vision of the great poets, but the learned and fantastic love of European tradition, the *Amour Courtois*, which was first shaped into art for modern Europe in Provence and found a home in all the languages of Christendom wherever a refined society and the practice of poetry met together. In Irish, too, it is clearly the poetry of society. To prove this, we need only point to the names of some of the authors . . . in Scotland, the Earl and Countess of Argyll and Duncan Campbell of Glenorquhy, 'the good knight', who died at Flodden'.

'A long farewell to yesternight! soon or late though it passed away. Though I were doomed to be hanged for it, would that it were this coming night!
There are two in this house tonight from whom the eye does not hide their secret; though they are not lip to lip, keen, keen is the glancing of their eyes.
Silence gives meaning to the swift glancing of the eyes; what avails the silence of the mouth when the eye makes a story of its secret?
Och, the hypocrites won't allow a word to cross my lips, O slow eye! Learn then what my eye declares, you in the corner over there:—
"Keep this night for us tonight; alas that we are not like this for ever! Do not let the morning in, get up and put the day outside."
Ah, Mary, graceful mother, Thou who art chief over all poets, help me, take my hand—a long farewell to yesternight!'

As a contrast to these, we can quote verses from a panegyric composed by a member of the same family, Cathal MacMhuirich, in the previous century. They are from an elegy for four chiefs of Clanranald who all died in 1636.

'Our rivers are without abundance of fishing, there is no hunting in the devious glens, there is little crop in every tilth, the wave has gnawed to the very base of the peaks. For their sake the fury of the ocean never ceases, every sea lacks jetsam on its shore; drinking wine at the time of carousal, the warriors grieve more than the women . . . Their survivors are gloomy and wrathful; the song of the cuckoos is not heard, the wind has taken on a senseless violence, the stream washes away its banks over the heather. Because the men of Glenranald have gone from us we poets cannot pursue our studies; it is time for the chief bard to depart after them, now that presents to poets will be abolished . . .'

The hyperbole of this and similar elegies is rooted in the ancient and universal belief that connects the life of a ruler with the fertility of his land. Earlier still, in the last quarter of the 15th century, when the Lordship of the Isles, from which Clanranald sprang, was under attack, we find the anxiety expressed that if Clan Donald, 'the brilliant pillars of green Alba', is destroyed, learning will be destroyed also.

'It is no joy without Clan Donald; it is no strength to be without them; the best race in the round world; to them belongs every good man . . .
In the van of Clan Donald learning was commanded, and in their rear were service and honour and self-respect . . .'

The anxiety was well founded, as history was to prove. Yet in spite of wholesale destruction of manuscripts when these learned orders were destroyed, enough has survived of their work, not only in poetry and history and romance, but also in law, medicine, astronomy—not to mention other more arcane pursuits—to show what a rich and varied world existed behind the clouds of political and military turbulence that for most people represents the 'history' of Gaelic Scotland.

Long before that world came to an end, however, the poets who composed in vernacular Gaelic had inherited its basic social and political attitudes and were able to draw freely on the resources of imagery developed by their classical brethren. In the late 16th and early 17th centuries the upper social reaches of vernacular poetry are inhabited by professional bards and members of leading clan families alike. Its range is quite unrestricted and eventually represents all grades of society, who expressed themselves in a wide variety of stanzaic and metrical patterns. Even the Latin-derived, syllable-counting measures of the classical poets are used with subtlety and ease as early as the 16th century: the Ossianic ballads upon which James MacPherson based his 'Ossian' belong formally to this sector and they too carry on a classical Gaelic inheritance into oral tradition, where they are now on the verge of extinction. But hundreds of thousands of lines, in both classical and colloquial Gaelic, have been preserved.

The classical inheritance thus gives modern Gaelic poetry metrical resources, in the subtle blend of stressed and syllabic verse, comparable to that produced by the fusion of French and Anglo-Saxon measures in English poetry. A demotic syllable-counting verse, with its quiet, tentative movement, is often used for religious and elegiac poetry. The emphasis, however, ought not to be laid so much on choice of subject associated with a particular metrical form as on the relationship between form and its associated rhetorical technique. Some have a rhythmic exuberance, some are exploratory and unhurried, others are abrupt and declamatory. Almost all of this poetry is sung; and in that connection it is relevant to recall W. P. Ker's dictum: 'The difference is in the tune, and it is a difference of thought as well.'

Especially declamatory are the ancient rhythmical metres which ante-date the introduction of Christianity and Latin learning and which survived in a modified form though still patently native. The primary function of these particular forms lies in clan panegyric, where the stress is on survival of the group of aristocratic warrior hunters at the top of society. The diction is codified in sets of conventional images, most densely concentrated in the heroic elegy composed at the point of crisis brought about by the death of a leader—in other words, when it is most necessary to reaffirm the traditional values of the community. One of the stock conventions of this praise-poetry is to rehearse the allies—real or ideal—of a clan. This is developed in poems associated with the 18th century Jacobite Risings. For instance, a poem of 1715 opens by referring to a prophecy (attributed to Thomas the Rhymer) that the Gaels will come into their own again in Scotland: this messianic hope of the disinherited is here firmly pinned on the Jacobite cause, and the poet draws up a formidable list of clans, including those who could not possibly be expected to support Jacobitism. But it is appropriate to note that the bards of Hanoverian clans were pro-Jacobite, clearly unaffected by the political and religious motives that put their chiefs on the Government side. And in view of the popular identification made between Jacobitism and Roman Catholicism, it is worth pointing out that it is a Protestant poet who puts forward the strongest arguments on behalf of the '45.

The attempts on the part of poets to preserve at least a conceptual Gaelic unity, a sense of nationhood, were successful up to a point, but at a price. The conventions of panegyric became a pervasive style. The style in turn reflects an attitude towards the world, which is regarded intellectually in terms of praise versus dispraise. Through genealogy it works into love poetry; it extends also to nature poetry, evoking a sense of friendly or unfriendly territory: in short, it bears the Gaelic sense of social psychology, of history, of geography. Although 'panegyric' in this context is only a framework, which allows the imagination a great deal of freedom, it seeks to institutionalise the creative mind and in the end became a straitjacket.

Through clan poems the social and political values of Gaelic society find expression. This strand is the Apollonian poetry of Gaelic, discoursing in a highly deliberate and intellectually controlled manner on issues that affect the clan or the nation: an example is the poem against the Union of the Parliaments in 1707.

At the other end of the poetic spectrum we find the Dionysian poetry that has survived largely in songs used to accompany various forms of communal labour. The majority were composed by women and transmitted in a predominantly female environment: more than one strain in the tradition seems to derive from an exclusively female sub-culture not necessarily connected with work—accompaniment to dance is a possibility. Indeed, their strong, almost hypnotic rhythms give the impression of belonging to an ecstatic ceremony. Their poetry unfolds, not in a smooth linear movement, but unevenly, with quite unpredictable changes in focus. But however disconcerting this may at times be, it is precisely these abrupt transitions from image to image, governed only by the nature of the situation expressed in the poem, that release the creative energy. These songs use language according to a principle which is at the farthest extreme from that of the logical, ordered sequences of prose. Out of this kaleidoscope of images, fusing and separating in oral transmission, certain more permanent forms were from time to time created—for example, the great anonymous poem by a girl to her dead lover Seathan. It ends thus:

'But Seathan is tonight in the upper homestead
Neither gold nor tears will win him
Neither drink nor music will tempt him
Neither slaughter nor violence will bring him from his doom . . .
Dear Seathan, dear Seathan,
I would not give you to law or king
I would not give you to mild Mary
I would not give you to the Holy Rood
I would not give you to Jesus Christ
For fear I would not get you myself.
O Seathan, my brightness of the sun!
Alas! despite me death has seized you,
And that has left me sad and tearful,
Lamenting bitterly that you are gone;
And if all the clerics say is true,
That there is a Hell and a Heaven,
My share of Heaven—it is my welcome to death—
For a night with my darling
With my companion, brown-haired Seathan.'

These tender, intensely passionate songs with their elemental themes provide the main lyrical impulse of Gaelic poetry. They have sometimes been compared with the Scots ballads, for the Ballad starkness is there, often enough. But they lack the supernatural element of the ballads: they are very much poems of this world, and their measure is the measure of a man.

The 17th century, to which most of the vernacular poetry we have touched on belongs, is exceedingly rich in various traditional forms. When we come to the 18th century, we enter an age of innovation and individual achievement. Alexander MacDonald, the great poet of the '45, was the first person to have a volume of secular poetry published—in 1751. MacDonald was a university man, aware of the wider political and literary issues of the mid-18th century, and he deliberately extended the scope of Gaelic poetry. This he achieved partly by structural means, partly by borrowing from James Thomson and Allan Ramsay and allowing the grafts to take up the vitality of an old Gaelic stock; for instance, in nature poetry. But it is his own native intellectual power and exuberance that gives his genius its force. Of no other Scottish poet can it be said with greater truth that he was possessed by *perfervidum ingenium Scottorum*. His influence was immense. His innovations were rapidly assimilated by contemporaries and successors, some of them illiterate; but so sophisticated is their art that MacDonald's formal learning gives him no advantage over non-literate poets like Duncan Bàn Macintyre in Argyll or Rob Donn in Sutherland. Rob Donn is on the northern boundary of the Gaelic world, psychologically as well as geographically removed from the influence of the Lordship of the Isles and from the panegyric tradition. For that and other reasons, among them the influence of Alexander Pope in Gaelic translation, his poetry of censure is not in the tradition of splendid invective but has the true, and very rare, satirical humour. Duncan Macintyre, doubtless following MacDonald's example, had his poetry written down for him and published in book form. His masterpiece, *The Praise of Ben Dorain* is a poem of extraordinary sophistication and sensibility, realising physical nature with a bold sweep of perception but also with a minute, precise, sensual delicateness: the lines of the landscape, the movement of deer, the qualities of the vegetation of the moor. It is a visual documentary, invented before the camera. Duncan Bàn is buried in Greyfriars Churchyard in Edinburgh, but he is still remembered in Highland oral tradition: an invariably genial, easy-going man. Tradition also preserves, perhaps as a counter-weight, the memory of William Ross as the poet who became so anguished and obsessed with a love affair that he wasted away physically to the dimensions of a child. He did in fact die at 28, apparently from tuberculosis, and his love poems are among the finest in all Gaelic. Finally, in the 18th century, Dugald Buchanan of Perthshire is regarded as the most powerful religious poet. His poetry has a terrible austerity: the flame of his compassion barely perceptible in the blinding light of the justice of God. He was a Presbyterian but his 'Day of Judgement' is in the great European tradition of the 'Dies Irae'. These poems are early documents of the Evangelical Revival that was soon to sweep through the entire Highlands and Islands.

Religious poets of the 18th century were the first to protest forcefully against the tyranny of landlords. The next century was the bitter century of the Clearances, when the chaos that the break-up of any traditional society produces was intensified beyond endurance in the bewilderment of a people attacked by their own natural leaders. This broken community eagerly accepted the demands of a passionate and uncompromising faith. It was a new dialectic, powerful enough to replace the deep loyalties of the traditional order, in which not religion but genealogy had been the opiate of the people. Predictably, the Evangelical Revival is bound up with social protest, but since the religion was other-worldly, essentially recluse although practised in open society, it could scarcely yield an adequate strategy from the full range of human experience. And so Gaelic poetry in the 19th and early 20th centuries is a strange amalgam: the unsettled complex of a transitional age. Partly for that very reason, it is much less dull and trivial than it has often been represented as being. It is sometimes nostalgic and anachronistic, still limited by the stereotype of panegyric. It goes off in false directions that could lead to nothing but sentimentality, as when it borrows from English or Scots and reproduces weak and prettified aspects of Romanticism. (This is not the only stage of Scottish history at which parallels can be drawn between Gaelic and Lowland traditions, but here the parallel is very obvious.) Yet it is still instinct with the old, splendid craftsmanship and there is a palpable widening and deepening of human sympathy. There are contrasts and oppositions almost at every turn, and they serve to remind us that we are dealing not with one simple strand but with what is still the art of a nation, no matter how attenuated. One vivid contrast, one that might be made a symbol of that age, is provided by the poetry of two MacLeod brothers from Skye: Neil, the reputable author of a highly popular book of poems, a fine, if limited, craftsman whose work almost always tended toward the pretty and sentimental; John, composer of songs in an oral tradition, a sailor and wanderer all his life, a poet of strong, realistic, compassionate poetry, the polarities of which are rooted in the life of Skye and the brutality of life in the sailing ships. John MacLeod was a bohemian trickster, who apparently had strong hypnotic powers; Neil MacLeod was a respectable gentleman and an honoured member of his community.

Contrasts of a different kind emerge in the poetry of Mary MacPherson, the poetess of the radical Land League agitation. In a dialogue poem composed after the flood-tide of the Evangelical Revival had reached Skye and all the pleasures of this world had become vanity, she makes a friend say:

'The people have become so strange
That sorrow to them is wheat
And if you will not go into a whelk-shell for them
You will not be able to stay alive.'

Her own reply comes abruptly:

'We will not go into a whelk-shell for them
And we will be able to stay alive:
Although we will not wear long faces
Nor cause our appearance to change . . .'

She thanks her friend for her good advice and adds:

'Since vanity is a plant that satisfies the flesh, it sticks to me as closely as the thong does to the shoe.' (Probably the old, home-made shoe in which the thong was part of the upper.)

In that climate she could not escape conscience searching. But she had come to terms with herself and had elected to remain robustly of this world, albeit with a strong religious sense of ultimate justice. Her introspection borrows from religion but never turns morbid. She had undergone a harrowing experience of unjust conviction and imprisonment for theft; it was this 'that brought my poetry into being', and the anguish of it remained ardent in her until the end of her life. She had, too, an intense affection for her native community. All these elements combine in her work, resolved and integrated and given a major dimension by being set in the context of 19th century Radicalism. She had indeed a perverse strain of panegyric (for instance, a 'Song for the Duke of Sutherland'!) which a fuller criticism would take into account. Yet her best work gives the sharp feel of immediate experience while at the same time conveying the pressure of contemporary events. And when she exults that 'We have seen the horizon breaking, the clouds of serfdom dispelled' she is inaugurating a new vision of Gaelic society.

From the 19th century onwards the outside world was invading the Gaelic consciousness with a cataclysmic effect. The Clearances are usually taken as the prime symbol, but equally destructive in its devastating psychological impact was the imposition of compulsory English education. The 1872 Act abolished the literacy that Gaelic schools had provided, often for monoglot Gaelic speakers. In these circumstances, it is extraordinary that any serious or sophisticated literature survives at all—or rather it would be, were it not for the maintenance of an intellectual tradition and the sense of cultural identity that poetry, very largely circulating orally, kept alive.

The 20th century witnessed an extraordinary revival. Once again, the parallel with the Lowlands may be noted. John Munro, a university graduate, killed in action in 1918 would certainly, on the promise of the few poems that survived from the trenches of France, have emerged as a major figure. But Sorley Maclean and George Campbell Hay in the Thirties, and Derick Thomson in the Fifties, are the major figures of the movement so far, though there are a number of other writers, in prose as well as poetry, who are currently extending the tradition. If one were to look for poetic ancestors for the trio mentioned, Munro would have a place in Thomson's genealogy and Mary MacPherson in Maclean's while Campbell Hay's ancestry stretches back to the poets of classical Gaelic. But that of course is only one aspect: these are contemporary 20th century poets whose best poetry is of European stature.

The foregoing account scarcely traces even the salient features of the tradition that they have inherited. It omits, for example, the great collection of charms and incantations and verse prayers that have been published under the title of *Carmina Gadelica*. Most of them are an extraordinary blend of paganism and Christianity: in some, 'paganism' is no more than an academic term, as in these prayers to the sun and moon.

'Greetings to you, sun of the seasons, as you travel the skies on high, with your strong steps on the wing of the heights; you are the happy mother of the stars.
You sink down in the perilous ocean without harm and without hurt, you rise up on the quiet wave like a young queen in flower.'

And:

'Greeting to you, new moon, kindly jewel of guidance! I bend my knees to you, I offer you my love.
I bend my knees to you, I raise my hands to you, I lift up my eyes to you, new moon of the seasons . . .
You journey on your course, you steer the flood-tides, you light up your face for us, new moon of the seasons.
Queen of guidance, queen of good luck, queen of my love, new moon of the seasons.'

Nor is there space to discuss the epigrams and verse adages that are sometimes reminiscent of the Greek Anthology: 'Better is weariness of the legs after a splendid deed than apathy and weariness of spirit; weariness of the legs lasts only an hour, weariness of the spirit lasts for ever.' Frequently verses of such a kind appear in the margins of manuscripts: Gaelic scribes were incorrigibly human. It may be the briefest of comments, like this 'paradign of a sigh', as it has been aptly described: 'Och, uch, ach, Olivia, it's all right for you!' jotted down when the writer should have been concentrating his attention elsewhere. So, too, as it were in the margins of oral traditions there are stray stanzas, fragments perhaps of longer poems: they wander in the mind, seeking fresh contexts:

'I saw a phantom ship last night
A light of death and dread at her mast
And I knew that my young and only son
Was dead beneath the paw of yonder sea'

Or by a woman:

'I gave love of such a kind
As would bind the stone without lime
As would send the great ship on the sea
To the heather's crest before she'd stop.'

Indicating the main lines of a tradition of necessity turns the attention away from so much of the individual genius: Anna Campbell's lament, for instance, for her drowned lover. It is of the late 18th century, but in her distracted grief she calls up an image of a practice that Edmund Spenser mentions in Ireland.

'I would drink a drink in spite of my kinsfolk
Not of the red wine of Spain
But the blood of your body—to me a better drink.'

We have also to set aside the idiosyncratic, the unexpected quirk of sensibility, the unique quality of imagination such as we find, for example, in the poetry of the obscure Donald of the Lays, son of Finlay who lived about 1600. To him is ascribed a long poem (perhaps a cycle of poems) known as 'The Song of the Owl of Strone', set in the landscape round Ben Nevis. It celebrates mountains and deer-hunting with hounds. It is also concerned with great men, the passage of time, old age, and with many other topics besides. To use Auden's terms, it is full of Sacred Events; and because that ultimate reach of the imagination has been attained, it is simultaneously mundane, vibrant, unmystical, and limitless. The observation in it is a kind of obsessive regard; which at times finds expression in a curious understatement: what emerges has a powerful, disturbing eloquence. But it is much too complex and mysterious to summarise here.

In this century, and particularly in the last twenty years, a tradition of drama has begun to flourish. An annual Gaelic Drama Festival is held in Glasgow, where the movement had its beginnings; significantly, more plays in Gaelic are now being performed at local festivals within the Gaelic speaking area. The lack of an indigenous dramatic tradition has often been commented on. To some extent, this reflects the rural nature of Gaelic society, the lack of urban centres which might have fostered it. Thus we have no record of mystery and miracle plays. In the period of the Evangelical Revival, the Church itself, particularly in its great open-air communion festivals, satisfied a need for drama.

But there did exist ancient traditions of mumming, associated with Hallowe'en, Christmas, Easter, and with festivals of saints such as St. Bride and St. Michael. They had been given a Christian dress, but they are clearly founded on fertility ceremonies. In the usual manner of such activities, from being performed by adults they developed into children's entertainment. There is one other scrap of information. In 1764 the minister of Glenelg tells that 'The Highlanders, at their festivals and other public meetings, acted the poems of Ossian. Rude and simple as their manner of acting was, yet any brave or generous action, any injury or distress, exhibited in the representation, had a surprising effect towards raising in them corresponding passions and sentiments.' (Interestingly enough the late Professor W. L. Renwick found what might have been the last vestige of dramatic production of Scots ballads in his own Border tradition.) Such evidence as we have, then, suggests strongly that only accidents of history prevented these rudimentary forms from developing.

At all events it is true to say that the main thrust of Gaelic genius has been in poetry, not in drama nor in prose. There is, of course, a prose tradition, and although it has its disjunctions, a case could be made out for its continuity from classical Gaelic on substantially the same grounds as those advanced by R. W. Chambers for English. In other words, the ecclesiastical influence is paramount: the church is the only public, social institution in which Gaelic is used. The finest prose of all has been lost beyond recall, for it consisted of the extempore sermons and prayers of the Evangelical Revival. Most 18th and 19th century written prose showed ecclesiastical influences of a more moderate and constricting nature; only in the last few decades do we see the steady growth of a more demotic kind. There is one large exception to that, however, in the folktales that have been written down from oral recitation.

For our purposes, we may discount short stories, essays, novels, etc., for the simple reason that they are not available in translation, whereas there are several collections of tales, with English summaries or full translations, dating from the 1860's onwards. This sector of Gaelic literature shares some features with that of poetry. There are an appreciable number of mediaeval romances which through being read aloud to a semi-literate or completely non-literate audience passed into and survived in oral, colloquial Gaelic. These tales have many of the characteristics of general European mediaeval romance: there are quests and perilous journeys to strange lands, supernatural adversaries, and the like. A large section consists of 'Fenian' stories, concerned with the exploits of Finn mac Coul (Fionn mac Cumhaill) and his warriors; Oisean, from which 'Ossian' is derived, is the son of Fionn and the poet of this warrior band in the tales and ballads.

Since there is available a useful short introduction* to Scottish Gaelic folktales, it is unnecessary to list all the categories. One consists of stories that are known the world over—the International Tales as folklorists call them. Versions of these may be found in Greek mythology, in Sanskrit literature, in collections of popular tales throughout the world, or in English literature, e.g. in Chaucer or Shakespeare. One may still hear the story of the Taming of the Shrew, for instance, in Gaelic, or come across the judgement of Portia and the pound of flesh. 'Three strips of flesh from his back and not one drop of blood to be spilt' as the Gaelic has it. Or it may be a localised tale of William Tell, or the Legend of Faust. Professor Kenneth Jackson writes about a visit to a storyteller in Uist: '. . . listening to the story with the sound of the Atlantic in my ears and the crest of St. Kilda on the horizon it was hard to believe that the first episode occurs in the pseudo-Homer, the main body is in an early Icelandic saga, and the last motif has affinities with an episode in Herodotus'.

The story in question was a Novella: these are realistic narratives which quite often introduce the theme of 'poor boy marries rich girl'. They have a wide range, and may borrow from unexpected sources; one very long novella from Benbecula is obviously indebted to *Robinson Crusoe*!

Finally there is one group, and a large one, which is at the farthest remove from the 'Fairytale' type of story and which in certain respects stands alone. These are the historical legends, or more precisely, clan sagas; they are short, many of them no more than anecdotes, and deal with the exploits of the leaders of that society and with feuds between different clans. They sometimes contain elements of the supernatural, not of the extravagant fairytale kind but drawn from the store of traditional

*K. H. Jackson 'The Folktale in Gaelic Scotland' in *Proceedings of the Scottish Anthropological and Folklore Society*, vol. iv (1952), pp. 123–140.

belief in second-sight and other eerie manifestations and portents. They are certainly founded on historical events and may contain factual information unknown elsewhere; even when they do not, they throw an incidental light on Gaelic attitudes. Almost invariably they are strong, vivid, dramatic narratives reminding us often of the qualities that make the Icelandic sagas so memorable. This extends even to dialogue. We read how the Icelandic warrior, thrust through the body by a spear in the doorway, turns round and observes: 'These broad-bladed spears are becoming fashionable', and it comes vividly before our minds when we hear of an incident in a feud between MacIain of Ardnamurchan and the Camerons.

> 'MacIain raised his helmet then and uncovered his forehead. There were two men of the Camerons opposite him, on the other side of a small stream.
> 'How nicely an arrow would alight on MacIain's brow!' said one of them.
> 'That is true,' said the other, 'but it is not your wavering eye nor your unsteady hand that could do it.'
> The first man was nettled at that. He took careful aim and slipped the arrow. It struck MacIain between the two eyes. MacIain seized the arrow and tore it out of the wound. As it came out the barb of the arrow ripped the artery and the blood gushed forth.
> "Was that a cleg that bit me?" he asked. Then he fell to the ground and died.'

There is frequently an incident, a mannerism, a physical peculiarity, that identifies a person while he is still far off. Usually it acts as a pivot in the development of the action.

Paul of the Thong in North Uist was given that name because he helped to kill Donald of Harris. Donald's brothers knew that they could not kill Donald except by treachery. They arranged to meet to engage in feats of strength and agility. One of the feats involved leaping through the door of a barn where Paul had been positioned. When Donald of Harris tried the feat, Paul flung a noose round his neck and hanged him in the doorway.

Donald's wife was pregnant and fled to Skye where she bore a son. This became known in Uist. One autumn day, many years later, when Paul and some other men were harvesting, a figure appeared on the skyline. Paul asked at once who it was; they watched him approach but nobody recognised him. Then Paul asked: 'Which way is the wind today?' They told him. Suddenly Paul said: 'If I am not mistaken that is the bouncing step of Angus, son of Donald of Harris!' and he fled, making for the nearest church sanctuary. The stranger, who was indeed Angus, pursued him, overtook him before he got to the sanctuary boundary, and there he killed Paul of the Thong.

That is the barest summary. It is given merely to indicate the tacit power of such legends. Here we have depicted a doomed man who for some twenty years has lived in constant fear, knowing that some day or some night the avenger of blood will appear. His ultimate fate is certain. When nobody can identify the stranger immediately for him, he asks about the wind. What he is concerned with is whether a ship could have sailed from Skye. And he has clearly taken the trouble to find out in detail about the man who is honour bound to take up the blood feud on behalf of his murdered father. He is able thus to identify him himself, from a peculiarity of gait. All this is transmitted with absolute clarity in a few brief phrases.

There is another story which illustrates much the same point but adds a sinister touch. It concerns the avenging of the Heirs of Keppoch. The story is quite long and involved, with a number of dramatic incidents.

A party of Clanranald MacDonalds had come from Uist to Lochaber in order to kill the men who had murdered the rightful heirs of Keppoch. The murderers only came occasionally to Keppoch House since they too knew that the law of the vendetta was inexorable. When the Clanranald men arrived they seized the cowherd but spared his life on condition that he would betray the murderers' presence whenever they came. The signal was to be a cattle-call from a nearby knoll. When the murderers eventually appeared, the cowherd waited until the evening milking, grabbed one of the girls and would let her go only if she promised that she would call a certain cow by name from the knoll.

' "Why?" asked the girl.

"Because when I hear you calling that cow *Blàrag* it seems to me that you have the loveliest head-voice that ever I heard."

Then he let her go. The girl stood on top of the knoll. *Blàrag*! *Blàrag*! *Blàrag*! she would call. And then she would laugh.'

That doom-laden, innocent laugh is hard to forget. From this point the story moves relentlessly towards its foreordained conclusion.

We said earlier that Gaelic literature had been cut off from the great innovating movements of post-medieval Europe. That this is largely true, at least until the present century, will now be clear. Equally it ought to be clear that it is not completely a local growth but has direct and indirect links with a much greater world. A close study of its rhetorical structures would demonstrate that beyond possibility of doubt, but it must suffice to draw attention to one figure. There is no more characteristic image of the literatures of mediaeval Europe than that of the Wheel of Fortune, fixed in the imagination of succeeding generations by Boethius in *De Consolatione Philosophiae*. That this image is a commonplace also of Gaelic poetry, and that it may appear in a song composed in a Hebridean township today, makes an eloquent comment. The continuing neglect of such a fascinating literature is a sad phenomenon of Scottish education.

# Gaelic Texts in Translation

## Section I: Folktales

| | |
|---|---|
| CAMPBELL, John F. | Popular tales of the West Highlands, volumes 1–4.<br>Published in Edinburgh, 1860–1862.<br>(Republished for Islay Association by Gardener.) |
| MacKAY, J. G. | More West Highland tales.<br>Vol. I, 1940.<br>Vol. II, 1960.<br>Oliver & Boyd. |
| MacKECHNIE, John | The Dewar manuscripts.<br>Vol. I,<br>Maclellan (Glasgow), 1964. |

## Section II: Songs

| | |
|---|---|
| CAMPBELL, John L. | Highland songs of the Forty-Five.<br>John Grant (Edinburgh), 1923. |
| CAMPBELL, John L. *and* COLLINSON, F. | Hebridean folksongs.<br>Oxford University Press, 1969. |

## Section III: Translations of Gaelic Poetry

| | |
|---|---|
| JACKSON, Kenneth H. | A Celtic miscellany. (1951). Penguin, 1971. |
| MacDONALD, A. & A. | The poems of Alexander MacDonald. Published in Inverness, 1924. |
| SINTON, Thomas | The poetry of Badenoch. The Northern Counties Publishing Company, 1906. |
| SMITH, Iain Crichton | Ben Dorain. Akros, 1969. |

## Section IV: Contemporary Gaelic Poetry

\* Denotes prose translations of *some* texts.

| | |
|---|---|
| HAY, George Campbell | *Fuaran Sléibh. 1947. *O na Ceithir Airdean. 1952. |
| MACAULAY, Donald | *Seóbhrach ás a' Chlaich. |
| MACLEAN, Sorley | *Dàin do Eimhir. Maclellan, 1943. Poems to Eimhir. Translations by I. Crichton Smith. Gollancz, 1971. *Northern House, 1971. Lines Review No. 34. Macdonald. |
| THOMSON, Derick | *An Dealbh Briste. 1951. *Eadar Samhradh is Foghar. 1967. The far road. New Rivers Press, 1971. |
| Four points of a Saltire | (Translations by Sorley Maclean, George Campbell Hay and William Neill of their own poetry.) Reprographia, 1970. |

## Section V

| | |
|---|---|
| THOMSON, Derick S. | An introduction to Gaelic poetry. Gollancz, 1974. |

# Booklists and Other Aids

Items selected for inclusion in these lists will, we believe, be useful in school. Among them, however, are many out-of-print items. They are included in the hope that a demand for them might be created, and that publishers will re-issue some of them.

# Scottish Literature: Selection of General Works

DAICHES, David
The paradox of Scottish culture: the eighteenth-century experience.
O.U.P., 1964. (o.p.)

GIBBON, L. G. *and* MacDIARMID, H.
Scottish scene. (1934)
Chivers, 1974.

LINDSAY, Maurice
Scotland: an anthology.
Robert Hale, 1974.

SPEIRS, John
The Scots literary tradition. 2nd ed.
Faber, 1962. (o.p.)

WITTIG, Kurt
The Scottish tradition in literature. (1958)
Greenwood Press, 1972.

WOOD, H. Harvey
Scottish Literature.
Longmans Green for the British Council, 1952. (o.p.)

**British Council series: Writers and Their Work (Longman):**

COLLINS, P. A. W.
Boswell, 1956.

DAICHES, David
Burns, 1957.

GASCOYNE, David
Carlye, 1957.

GREENLEES, Douglas
Norman Douglas, 1957.

PARKER, W. M.
Susan Ferrier and John Galt, 1965.

YOUNG, K.
Compton MacKenzie, 1968.

JACK, Ian
Sir Walter Scott, 1958.

BRANDER, Laurence
Smollett, 1957.

STUBBS, Patricia
Muriel Spark, 1973.

STERN, G. B.
Stevenson, 1952.

WOOD, H. Harvey
Two Scots Chaucerians (Dunbar and Henryson), 1967.

# Novels

A date following a title indicates first publication. The date following the publisher indicates latest edition.

†Denotes a novel currently in use as class text.   *Denotes a paperback edition.

BARKE, James
The land of the leal. (1939)
Chivers, 1969.
The wind that shakes the barley. (1946)
*Fontana, 1975.

BARRIE, *Sir* J. M.
Farewell, Miss Julie Logan. (1931)
Hodder, 1970.
The little minister.
Cassell, 1891. (o.p.)
Sentimental Tommy.
Cassell, 1896. (o.p.)

BERMANT, Chaim I.
Ben preserve us.
*Mayflower, 1967. (o.p.)
Berl make tea.
Chapman & Hall, 1965. (o.p.)
*Mayflower, 1970. (o.p.)
Jericho sleep alone.
Chapman & Hall, 1964. (o.p.)

BLAKE, George
†The shipbuilders. (1935)
Collins, 1970.
*Pan, 1972.
The westering sun. (1946)
Lythway, 1971.

BROWN, George Mackay
Greenvoe.
Hogarth Press, 1972.
Magnus.
Hogarth Press, 1973.

BUCHAN, John,
1st Baron Tweedsmuir
†Greenmantle. (1916)
Hodder, 1957.
†Huntingtower. (1922)
Hodder, 1960

†Mr. Standfast. (1919)
Hodder, 1953.
†Prester John. (1910)
*Pan, 1972.
†The thirty-nine steps. (1915)
Dent, 1964.
Hodder, 1947.
Longman.
*Pan, 1967.
†The three hostages. (1924)
Hodder, 1959.
*U.L.P., 1952.
Witch Wood.
Hodder, 1927. (o.p.)

CAMPBELL, Marion
The dark twin.
Turnstone, 1973.

CRONIN, A. J.
The citadel. (1937)
*New English Library, 1968.
Hatter's castle. (1931)
*New English Library, 1970.
The keys of the kingdom. (1941)
*New English Library, 1968.
The stars look down. (1935)
*New English Library, 1965.

DOUGLAS, George, (pseud. of George Douglas Brown)
†The house with the green shutters. (1901)
*Holmes McDougall, 1974.

DUNNETT, Dorothy
The game of kings.
Cassell, 1963.
*Sphere, 1972.

FORD, James Allan
A judge of men.
Hodder, 1968. (o.p.)

F

A statue for a public place.
Hodder, 1965. (o.p.)

FRIEL, George
The boy who wanted peace. (1964)
*Calder & Boyars, 1967.
*Pan, 1972.
Mr Alfred, M. A. (1972)
*Calder & Boyars, 1973.

GALT, John
Annals of the parish. (1821)
*O.U.P., 1972.
The entail, or The lairds of Grippy. (1822)
O.U.P., 1970.
The provost. (1822)
Chivers, 1968.
O.U.P., 1973.
Ringan Gilhaize, or The covenanters. (1823)
(o.p.)

GIBBON, Lewis Grassic (pseud. of James
Leslie Mitchell)
†A Scots quair. (1932–4; 1946)
Hutchinson, 1974.
*Pan, 1973. (3 volumes)
†Spartacus. (1933)
Hutchinson, 1970.
†Sunset song. (1932)
*Longman, 1971.

GUNN, Neil Miller
Butcher's broom.
Porpoise Press, 1934. (o.p.)
The green isle of the great deep.
Faber, 1944. (o.p.)
†Highland river. (1937)
Hutchinson, 1974.
*Arrow Books, 1974.
†Morning tide.
Faber, 1931. (o.p.)
†The silver darlings. (1941)
*Faber, 1969.

HANLEY, Clifford
†The taste of too much. (1960)
Blackie, 1967.

HAY, John Macdougall
Gillespie. (1914)
Duckworth, 1963. (o.p.)

HIND, Archie
The dear green place.
Hutchinson, 1966. (o.p.)

HOGG, James
The private memoirs and confessions of a
justified sinner. (1824)
O.U.P., 1969.
*O.U.P., 1970.

JENKINS, Robin
The changeling.
Macdonald, 1958. (o.p.)
Happy for the child. (1953)
Chivers, 1965.
So gaily sings the lark. (1950)
Chivers, 1971.

The Thistle and the Grail.
Macdonald, 1954. (o.p.)
A very Scotch affair.
Gollancz, 1968.

KENNAWAY, James
The cost of living like this.
Longman, 1969.
*Penguin, 1972.
Household ghosts. (1961)
Longman, 1969.
Silence.
Cape, 1972.
†Tunes of glory. (1956)
Transworld, 1960. (o.p.)

LINDSAY, David
A voyage to Arcturus. (1920)
Gollancz, 1968.
*Ballantine, 1972.

LINKLATER, Eric
Laxdale Hall.
Cape, 1951. (o.p.)
Magnus Merriman.
Cape, 1934. (o.p.)
The men of Ness.
Cape, 1932.
Private Angelo.
Cape, 1946.
White Maa's saga.
Cape, 1929. (o.p.)

MacARTHUR, Alexander, and LONG,
H. Kingsley
No mean city. (1935)
Spearman, 1956.
*Corgi, 1969.

MacCOLLA, Fionn (pseud. of T. Douglas
Macdonald)
The Albannach. (1932)
Reprographia, 1971.
And the cock crew.
Maclellan, 1945; Burns, 1962. (o.p.)
(Remaining stock purchased by Scotbooks,
Caithness.)
Scottish Noel.
Castle Wynd Printers, 1958. (o.p.)

McCRONE, Guy
Wax fruit.
Constable, 1947. (o.p.)

McILVANNEY, William
Docherty.
Allen & Unwin, 1975.
A gift from Nessus.
Eyre & Spottiswoode, 1968. (o.p.)
Remedy is none.
Eyre & Spottiswoode, 1966. (o.p.)

MacKENZIE, Compton
The monarch of the glen.
Chatto, 1941.
Sinister Street. (1913–14)
*Penguin, 1969.
Whisky Galore. (1947)
Chatto Educational, 1963.

MacNICOL, Eona
Colum of Derry.
Sheed & Ward, 1954. (o.p.)
Lamp in the night wind.
Sheed & Ward.
Maclellan, 1964.

MacPHERSON, Ian
Land of our fathers. (1933)
Chivers, 1965.

MARSHALL, Bruce
The black oxen.
Constable, 1972.
Father Malachy's miracle. (1931; 1948)
Constable, 1963.

MITCHISON, Naomi
The bull calves.
Cape, 1947. (o.p.)

MORRISON, Nancy Brysson
The gowk storm. (1933)
Chivers, 1968.

MUIR, Willa
Mrs. Ritchie.
Martin Secker, 1933. (o.p.)

MUNRO, Neil
John Splendid. (1899)
Blackwood, 1955.
†The new road. (1914)
Blackwood, 1969.

PATERSON, Neil
Behold thy daughter. (1950)
Hodder, 1973.

SCOTT, *Sir* Walter
The bride of Lammermoor. (1819)
*Dent.
Guy Mannering. (1815)
*Dent.
†The heart of Midlothain. (1818)
Collins, 1952.
*Dent.
†Old Mortality. (1816)
*Dent, 1969.
*Penguin, 1975.
†Redgauntlet. (1824)
*Dent, 1963.
†Rob Roy. (1817)
*Dent, 1963.
†Waverley. (1814)
*Dent, 1973.
*Penguin, 1972.

SHARP, Alan
A green tree in Gedde.
M. Joseph, 1965. (o.p.)
*New English Library, 1970.

SMITH, Iain Crichton
†Consider the lilies. (1968)
*Pergamon, 1970.
The last summer.
Gollancz, 1969. (o.p.)

SMOLLETT, Tobias
Humphry Clinker. (1771)
O.U.P., 1966.
*O.U.P., 1972.
*Penguin, 1971.

SPARK, Muriel
The ballad of Peckham Rye.
Macmillan, 1960.
*Penguin, 1970.
†The prime of Miss Jean Brodie.
Macmillan, 1961.
*Penguin, 1969.

STEVENSON, Robert Louis
†Catriona. (1892)
Nelson.
O.U.P.
†Kidnapped. (1886)
Longman, and others.
*Penguin, 1967.
†The Master of Ballantrae. (1889)
Dent, and others.
†The strange case of Dr Jekyll
and Mr Hyde. (1886)
*Dent, 1962.
†Treasure island. (1883)
Heinemann, 1964.
*Penguin, 1971.
†Weir of Hermiston. (1896)
*Holmes McDougall, 1973.

SUTHERLAND, Elizabeth
The seer of Kintail.
Constable, 1974.

URQUHART, Fred
Time will knit. (1938)
Chivers, 1969.

WILLIAMS, Gordon Maclean
From scenes like these. (1968)
*Mayflower, 1970.

# The Novel: Biographies and Critical Works

*Denotes a paperback edition.

## A. General Critical and Background Works dealing with (inter alia) the Novel

CRAIG, David
Scottish literature and the Scottish
people 1680–1830.
Chatto & Windus, 1961.

SPEIRS, John
The Scots literary tradition. 2nd ed.
Faber, 1962. (o.p.)

WITTIG, Kurt
The Scottish tradition in literature. (1958)
Greenwood Press, 1972.

## B. Individual Authors

BROWN (George
Douglas):
Veitch, James
George Douglas Brown.
Herbert Jenkins, 1952. (o.p.)

GALT:
Aberdein, J. W.
John Galt. O.U.P., 1936.
(o.p.)

Gordon, I. A.
John Galt: the life of a writer.
Oliver & Boyd, 1972

GIBBON:
Munro, I. S.
Leslie Mitchell: Lewis
Grassic Gibbon.
Oliver & Boyd, 1966. (o.p.)

Young, Douglas F.
Beyond the sunset.
Impulse Books, 1973.

GUNN:
Morrison, David, ed.
Essays on Neil M. Gunn.
Caithness Books, 1971.
*Caithness Books, 1971.

Scott, Alexander and
Gifford, Douglas, eds.
Neil Gunn: the man and
the writer.
Blackwood, 1973.

HOGG:
Batho, Edith C.
The Ettrick shepherd.
C.U.P., 1927. (o.p.)

Simpson, Louis
James Hogg: a critical study.
Oliver & Boyd, 1962. (o.p.)

MacCOLLA:
Morrison, David, ed.
Essays on Fionn MacColla.
Caithness Books, 1973.

SCOTT:
Bell, Alan, ed.
Scott bicentenary essays.
Scottish Academic Press 1973.

Buchan, John
Sir Walter Scott.
Cassell, 1932. (o.p.)

Clark, A. Melville
Sir Walter Scott: the
formative years.
Blackwood, 1969.

Cockshut, A. O. J.
The achievement of Sir
Walter Scott.
Collins, 1969. (o.p.)

Crawford, Thomas
Scott.
*Oliver & Boyd, 1965. (o.p.)

Daiches, David
Sir Walter Scott and his world.
Thames & Hudson, 1971.

Devlin, D. D.
The author of *Waverley*:
Sir Walter Scott.
Macmillan, 1971.

Mayhead, Robin
Walter Scott.
C.U.P., 1973.
*C.U.P., 1973.

Muir, E.
Scott and Scotland.
Routledge, 1936.

Oman, Carola
The Wizard of the North.
Hodder & Stoughton, 1973.

*STEVENSON:*     Daiches, David
[1]Stevenson and the art of
fiction.
New York, 1951. (o.p.)

[1]This 22-page lecture was privately printed in
New York.

Robert Louis Stevenson
and his world.
Thames & Hudson, 1973.

Eigner, Edwin M.
Robert Louis Stevenson and
romantic tradition.
Princeton U.P., 1967.

Furnas, J. C.
Voyage to windward: the life
of Robert Louis Stevenson.
Faber, 1952. (o.p.)

Hennessy, James Pope
Robert Louis Stevenson.
Cape, 1974.

Kiely, Robert
Robert Louis Stevenson and
the fiction of adventure.
Harvard U. P., 1965.

# Short Stories: Collections

*Denotes a paperback edition.

CAMPBELL, Angus, *ed.*
Scottish tales of terror.
*Fontana, 1972.

GIFFORD, Douglas, *ed.*
Scottish short stories, 1800–1900.
*Calder & Boyars, 1971.

HAINING, Peter, *ed.*
The clans of darkness: Scottish stories of
fantasy and horror.
Gollancz, 1971.
*Sphere, 1972.

HENDRY, J. F., *ed.*
The Penguin book of Scottish short stories.
*Penguin, 1970.

LINDSAY, M *and* URQUHART, F. *eds.*
No Scottish twilight.
Maclellan, 1947. (o.p.)

MILLAR, Robert *and* LOW, John T., *eds.*
Ten modern Scottish stories.
*Heinemann, 1973.

REID, James M., *ed.*
Scottish short stories.
O.U.P., 1963.

SCOTTISH ARTS COUNCIL
Scottish short stories. (pref. by N. Paterson)
Collins, 1973.
Scottish short stories, 1974. (pref. by C. Hanley)
Collins, 1974.

URQUHART, F. *ed.*
Scottish short stories.
Faber, 1957. (o.p.)

# Short Stories: Individual Authors

*Denotes a paperback edition.

BARRIE, *Sir*. J. M.
Auld licht idylls.
Hodder & Stoughton, 1888. (o.p.)
A window in Thrums.
Hodder & Stoughton, 1889. (o.p.)

BRISTER, Charles
This is my kingdom.
David Winter, 1972.

BROWN, George Mackay
A calendar of love, and other stories.
Hogarth Press, 1967.
Hawkfall.
Hogarth Press, 1974.
A time to keep.
Hogarth Press, 1969.

BROWN, John
Rab and his friends. (1858)
Dent, 1970.
*Dent, 1972.

BUCHAN, John, 1st Baron Tweedsmuir
The watcher by the threshold, and other tales.
Blackwood, 1902. (o.p.)

DAVIE, Elspeth
Spark and other stories.
Calder & Boyars, 1969.

GIBBON, Lewis Grassic (pseud. of James
Leslie Mitchell)
A Scots hairst.
Hutchinson, 1967.

GORDON, Giles
Pictures from an exhibition.
Allison & Busby, 1970.

GRAHAM, Robert Bontine Cunninghame
Rodeo.
Heinemann, 1936. (o.p.)
Scottish short stories.
Duckworth, 1914. (o.p.)

GUNN, Neil Miller
The white hour, and other stories.
Faber, 1950. (o.p.)

HAYNES, Dorothy K.
Thou shalt not suffer a witch, and other stories.
Methuen, 1949. (o.p.)

JAMIESON, Morley
The old wife, and other stories.
Macdonald, 1972.

MacNICOL, Eona K.
The Hallowe'en hero, and other stories.
Blackwood, 1969.

MUNRO, Neil
The lost pibroch, and other sheiling
stories. (1896)
Blackwood, 1929. (o.p.)
Para Handy tales. (1906–23)
Blackwood, 1963.
*Pan, 1969.

SCOTT, *Sir* Walter
Short stories.
O.U.P., 1934 (World's Classics) (o.p.)

SMITH, Iain Crichton
The black and the red.
Gollancz, 1973.
Survival without error.
Gollancz, 1970.

STEVENSON, Robert Louis
The tales of Tusitala.
Art & Educational Publishers, 1946. (o.p.)

TOULMIN, David
Hard shining corn.
Impulse Books, 1972.

URQUHART, Fred
The dying stallion.
Hart-Davis, 1967. (o.p.)
The ploughing match.
Hart-Davis, 1968. (o.p.)

# Drama: Full-Length Plays

*Denotes a paperback edition.

ARDEN, John
Armstrong's last goodnight.
Methuen, 1965.
*Methuen, 1965.

BARRIE, *Sir* J. M.
The admirable Crichton. (1902)
*U.L.P., 1967.
Dear Brutus. (1917)
U.L.P., 1962.
Mary Rose. (1920)
*Hodder, 1973.
Quality Street. (1902)
*French.
What every woman knows. (1908)
*French.

*All available in:*
The definitive edition of the plays of J. M. Barrie.
Hodder & Stoughton, 1942.

BOTTOMLEY, Gordon
Gruach.
Constable, 1921. (o.p.)

BRANDANE, John
Heather gentry.
Constable, 1932. (o.p.)
The glen is mine, *and* The lifting: two plays.
Constable, 1925. (o.p.)

BRIDIE, James
The anatomist.
*Constable, 1931.
The Baikie Charivari.
Constable, 1953. (o.p.)
Daphne Laureola.
*Constable, 1949.
Doctor Angelus.
*Constable, 1950.

The forrigan reel, in *John Knox and other plays.*
(1949)
Constable. (o.p.)
The golden legend of Shults, in *Susannah and the
elders, and other plays.* (1940)
Constable.
Mr Bolfry, in *Plays for plain people.*
Constable, 1944. (o.p.)
Mr Gillie.
*Constable, 1950.
A Sleeping Clergyman
*Constable, 1933.
Susannah and the elders.
*Constable, 1940. (hardback also)

BROWN, George Mackay
A spell for green corn.
Hogarth Press, 1970.

BRYDEN, Bill
Benny Lynch.
*Southside, 1975. (hardback also)
Willie Rough.
*Southside, 1972. (hardback also)

CONN, Stewart
The burning.
Calder & Boyars, 1973.

HOME, John
[1]Douglas. (1756)
*Oliver & Boyd, 1972. (hardback also)

KEMP, Robert
The King of Scots.
St. Giles Press, 1951. (o.p.)
Let wives tak tent.
Master John Knox.
Saint Andrew Press, 1960. (o.p.)

[1]Also appears under DRAMA: SPECIAL EDITIONS OR COLLECTIONS.

78

A nest of singing birds.
The other dear charmer.
Duckworth, 1957. (o.p.)

LINDSAY, *Sir* D.
[1]A satire of the three estates. (1540)
Heinemann, 1967.

McGRATH, John
The cheviot, the stag and the black, black oil.
*West Highland Publishing Company, 1974.

McLELLAN, Robert
The flouers o' Edinburgh. (1947)
[1]The hypocrite. (1967)
*Calder & Boyars, 1970. (hardback also)
[1]Jamie the Saxt. (1937)
*Calder & Boyars, 1970. (hardback also)
Toom byres. (1936)
Maclellan, 1947. (o.p.)
Torwatletie. (1946)
Maclellan, 1950. (o.p.)

MacMILLAN, Hector
The rising.
The royal visit.
The sash.
*Molendinar Press, 1974.

McMILLAN, Roddy
The bevellers.
*Southside, 1974. (hardback also)

RAMSAY, Allan
The gentle shepherd, in *Poems by* Allan Ramsay
and Robert Fergusson.
Scottish Academic Press, 1974.

REID, Alexander
Diana.
[1]The lass wi' the muckle mou'.
Voyage ashore.
The wax doll.
World without end.
[1]The world's wonder.
Collins, 1958. (o.p.)

RICHARDSON, Alan
Nicht o' the blunt claymore.
Brown, Son & Ferguson.

SCOTLAND, James
Cambusdonald Royal.
Brown, Son & Ferguson.
The honours of Drumlie.
Brown, Son & Ferguson.
Lucinda.
Brown, Son & Ferguson.
Lucy, Lucy, Lucy.
Brown, Son & Ferguson.
The sorcerer's tale.
Brown, Son & Ferguson.
Wild geese at midnight.
Brown, Son & Ferguson.

SCOTT, Alexander
Right royal.

SMITH, Sydney Goodsir
The Wallace.
Oliver & Boyd, 1960.

[1]Also appears under DRAMA: SPECIAL EDITIONS OR COLLECTIONS.

# Drama: Short Plays

*Denotes a paperback edition.

ADAM, Agnes
The bonesetter.
Brown, Son & Ferguson.
The old chest.
Brown, Son & Ferguson.

BARRIE, Sir J. M.
The twelve-pound look. (1910)
*French.

BLACK, C. Stewart
The guinea's stamp.
Brown, Son & Ferguson.
The Rajah of Riddrie.
Brown, Son & Ferguson.

BOTTOMLEY, Gordon
Choric plays.
Constable, 1939. (o.p.)
Culbin sands.
in *Lyric plays*. (1932) (o.p.)
The white widow.
in *Scottish one-act plays*, ed. J. M. Reid. (1938)

BRANDANE, John
Rory aforesaid. (1926)
in *Five Scottish one-act plays*, ed. Millar & Low.
*Heinemann, 1972.

BRIDIE, James
The amazed evangelist.
Constable, 1932. (o.p.)
The pardoner's tale. (1930)
in *Five Scottish one-act plays*, ed. Millar & Low.
*Heinemann, 1972.

CARRUTHERS, George S.
Highland fling.
Brown, Son & Ferguson.
Trouble brewing.
Brown, Son & Ferguson.
Wha's laird?
Brown, Son & Ferguson.

CARSWELL, Donald
Count Albany.
Dent. (o.p.)

CONN, Stewart
The king.
in *New English Dramatists 14*.
*Penguin, 1970.

CORRIE, Joe
The darkness. (1932)
Brown, Son & Ferguson.
Hewers of coal. (1937)
in *Five Scottish one-act plays*, ed. Millar & Low.
*Heinemann, 1972.
The hoose o' the hill.
French, 1932. (o.p.)

EVELING, Stanley
Come and be killed, *and* Dear Janet
Rosenberg, dear Mr Koonig.
*Calder & Boyars, 1971.

FERGUSON, J. A.
Campbell of Kilmohr. (1927)
in *Five Scottish one-act plays*, ed. Millar & Low.
*Heinemann, 1972.

FINLAY, Ian Hamilton
The estate hunters.
*Penguin.

GALLACHER, Tom
Mr Joyce is leaving Paris.
*Calder, 1972.

GUNN, Neil Miller
Back home.
Harrap, 1932. (o.p.)
Choosing a play: a comedy of community drama.
Porpoise Press, 1938. (o.p.)
also in *Scottish one-act plays*, ed. J. M. Reid.

JOHN, Evan
Prelude to massacre.
French, 1937. (o.p.)

KEMP, Robert
The asset.
St. Giles Press, 1952. (o.p.)
The deep freeze.
St. Giles Press. (o.p.)

McCABE, John
The friars of Berwick.
Brown, Son & Ferguson.

McLELLAN, R.
The changeling, 2nd rev. version.
Maclellan, 1950.
also in *Scottish one-act plays*, ed. J. M. Reid.
Porpoise Press, 1938. (o.p.)
Jeddart justice.
Bone & Hulley, 1934. (rev. ed. 194–). (o.p.)

MacVICAR, Angus
Mercy flight.
Brown, Son & Ferguson.

PATERSON, A. B.
Highland games.
Russell & Sons. (o.p.)

SCOTLAND, James
Baptie's lass.
Brown, Son & Ferguson.
The burning question.
Brown, Son & Ferguson.
The daurk assize.
Brown, Son & Ferguson.
The girl of the golden city.
Brown, Son & Ferguson.
Grand finale.
Brown, Son & Ferguson.
Hallowe'en.
Brown, Son & Ferguson.
Himself when young.
Brown, Son & Ferguson.
A surgeon for Lucinda.
Brown, Son & Ferguson.
Union riots.
Brown, Son & Ferguson.

SCOTT, Alexander
The last time I saw Paris.
Shetland yarn.
Untrue Thomas.
Caledonian Press, 195–. (o.p.)

WADDELL, George
The flesh and the devil.
Brown, Son & Ferguson.
Kirkpatrick's gowd.
Albyn Press. (o.p.)
The white cockade.
Brown, Son & Ferguson.

# Drama: Special Editions or Collections

\*Denotes a paperback edition.

BRIDIE, James
Tobias and the angel.
(Introduction & Notes by A. C. Ward)
\*Constable, 1931.

HOME, John
[1]Douglas. (1756)
(ed. Gerald D. Parker)
\*Oliver & Boyd, 1972. (hardback also)

LINDSAY, *Sir* David
Ane satyre of the thrie estaits. (1540)
(ed. James Kinsley)
Cassell, 1954. (o.p.)

LINDSAY, *Sir* David
[1]A satire of the three estates. (1540)
(ed. Matthew McDiarmid)
Heinemann, 1967.

McLELLAN, Robert
[1]The hypocrite. (1967)
\*Calder & Boyars, 1970. (hardback also)

[1]Jamie the Saxt. (1937)
(ed. Ian Campbell and Ronald Jack)
\*Calder & Boyars, 1971. (hardback also)

MILLAR, Robert *and* LOW, J. T. *eds.*
Five Scottish one-act plays:
    Campbell of Kilmohr
    Thread o' scarlet
    Rory aforesaid
    The pardoner's tale
    Hewers of coal
\*Heinemann, 1972.

REID, Alexander
[1]Two Scots plays: The lass wi' the muckle mou';
The world's wonder.
Collins, 1958. (o.p.)

REID, J. Macnair, *ed.*
Scottish one-act plays.
Porpoise Press, 1938. (o.p.)

[1]Also appears under DRAMA: FULL-LENGTH PLAYS.

# Drama: Critical Studies or Articles

BANNISTER, Winifred
James Bridie and his theatre.
Rockliff, 1955. (o.p.)

GERBER, Ursula
James Bridies dramen.
Bern, 1961.

LOW, J. T.
Scottish drama—the broukit bairn.
Article in *Teaching English*, Vol. 3, No. 3,
May, 1970.

LUYBEN, Helen L.
James Bridie: clown and philosopher.
University of Pennsylvania Press, 1966.

SMALL, Christopher
Scottish drama today.
A.S.L.S. Occasional Papers No. 1,
Scottish Writing Today, September, 1972.

WITTIG, Kurt
The Scottish tradition in literature. (1958)
Chapter X, Scottish drama.
Greenwood Press, 1972.

The Twelve seasons of the Edinburgh Gateway
Company 1953–65.
St. Giles Press, 1965.

# Poetry

*Denotes a paperback edition.

**A. Anthologies likely to be of use in the classroom:**

BRUCE, G. *ed.*
The Scottish literary revival: an anthology of twentieth-century poetry.
Collier-Macmillan, 1968. (o.p.)

BUCHAN, N. *ed.*
101 Scottish songs.
Collins, 1962.

BUCHAN, N *and* HALL, P. *eds.*
The Scottish folk singer.
*Collins, 1973.

GRAVES, R. *ed.*
English and Scottish ballads.
*Heinemann, 1967.

HODGART, M. *ed.*
The Faber book of ballads. (1965)
*Faber, 1971.

KING, C. *ed.*
Twelve modern Scottish poets.
*U.L.P., 1971.

LINDSAY, M. *ed.*
Modern Scottish poetry: an anthology of the Scottish Renaissance. 2nd ed. rev.
Faber, 1966. (o.p.) 3rd ed. in preparation.
Voices of our kind: an anthology of contemporary Scottish verse.
Saltire Society, 1971. New ed. in preparation.

MacCAIG, N. *and* SCOTT, A. *eds.*
Contemporary Scottish verse, 1959–1969.
*Calder & Boyars, 1970.

MacGILLIVRAY, A. *and* RANKIN, J. *eds.*
The ring of words: an anthology of Scottish poetry for secondary schools.
Oliver & Boyd, 1970. (o.p.)

MACKIE, R. L. *and* LINDSAY, M. *eds.*
A book of Scottish verse. 2nd ed.
O.U.P., 1967. (World's Classics)

MacMILLAN, A. *ed.*
The new Scots reader.
Oliver & Boyd, 1972.

Penguin Modern Poets, No. 21
(Crichton Smith, MacCaig, Mackay Brown)
*Penguin, 1972. (o.p.)

**B. Anthologies likely to be of use in the Library:**

BUCHAN, D. *ed.*
A Scottish ballad book.
Routledge & Kegan Paul, 1973.

BUCHAN, J. *ed.*
The Northern muse.
Nelson, 1924. (o.p.)

CHAMBERS, R. *ed.*
Popular rhymes of Scotland.
Chambers, 1870. (o.p.)

DIXON, W. Macneile *ed.*
The Edinburgh book of Scottish verse, 1300–1900.
Meiklejohn & Holden, 1910. (o.p.)

GARIOCH, R. *ed.*
Made in Scotland.
*Carcanet Press, 1974.

GLEN, D. *ed.*
The Akros anthology of Scottish poetry, 1965–70.
Akros, 1970.

GRAY, M. M. *ed.*
Scottish poetry from Barbour to James VI.
Dent, 1935. (o.p.)

GREIG, G. *and* KEITH, A. *eds.*
Last leaves of traditional ballads and
ballad airs.
Buchan Field Club, 1925. (o.p.)

KINGHORN, A. *ed.*
The Middle Scots poets.
*Arnold, 1970.

KINSLEY, J. *ed.*
The Oxford book of ballads.
O.U.P., 1969.

MacDIARMID, H. *ed.*
The golden treasury of Scottish poetry.
Macmillan, 1940. (o.p.)

MacQUEEN, J. *and* W. *eds.*
A choice of Scottish verse, 1470–1570.
*Faber, 1972.

MacQUEEN, J. *and* SCOTT, T. *eds.*
The Oxford book of Scottish verse.
O.U.P., 1966.

MARWICK, E. *ed.*
Anthology of Orkney verse.
Kirkwall Press, 1949.

MONTGOMERIE, N. *and* W. *eds.*
Scottish nursery rhymes.
Hogarth Press, 1975.

OLIVER, J. W. *and* SMITH, J. C. *eds.*
A Scots anthology.
Oliver & Boyd, 1947. (o.p.)

ORD, J. *ed.*
Bothy songs and ballads. (1930)
John Donald, 1973. (Scottish Reprint Library)

SARGENT, H. C. *and* KITTREDGE, G. L. *eds.*
English and Scottish popular ballads
(one-volume version of Child).
Harrap, 1922. (o.p.)
*F. J. Child's original work is available
in paperback in 5 volumes.*
Dover Publications, 1966.

SCOTT, R. I. *ed.*
From Barbour to Burns.
Blackie, 1960.

SCOTT, T. *ed.*
The Penguin book of Scottish verse.
*Penguin, 1970.
Late medieval Scots poetry: a selection
from the Makars.
Heinemann, 1967. (o.p.)

YOUNG, D. *ed.*
Scottish verse, 1851–1951.
Nelson, 1952. (o.p.)

Scottish poetry, Vols. 1–7.
1–6: Edinburgh University Press.
7: Glasgow University Press.

## C. School anthologies which contain a considerable number of Scottish poems:

RINTOUL, D. *and* SKINNER, J. *eds.*
Poet's quair.
Oliver & Boyd, 1950.

The Lanimer books of verse, Revised edition,
Vols. 2 & 3. Blackie.

SUMMERFIELD, G. *ed.*
Worlds: seven modern poets.
*Penguin, 1974.

## D. Major poets most likely to be of value:

BARBOUR, J.
The Bruce: a selection. (*ed.* A. M. Kinghorn)
Saltire, 1960.

BROWN, George Mackay
Poems new and selected.
Hogarth Press, 1971.
Fishermen with ploughs: a poem cycle.
Hogarth Press, 1971.

BURNS, R.
Poems and songs. (*ed.* J. Kinsley)
*O.U.P., 1971.
A choice of Burns's poems and songs.
(*ed.* S. G. Smith)
*Faber, 1966.
Selected poems. (*ed.* G. S. Fraser) (1960)
*Heinemann, 1968.
Poems. (*ed.* H. W. Meikle *and* W. Beattie)
*Penguin, 1972.

DAVIDSON, J.
A selection of his poems. (*ed.* M. Lindsay)
Hutchinson, 1961. (o.p.)
Poems. (*ed.* A. Turnbull) 2 vols.
Scottish Academic Press, 1973.

DUNBAR, W.
Poems. (*ed.* J. Kinsley)
*O.U.P., 1969.
Selected poems. (*ed.* H. MacDiarmid)
Saltire, 1952.

FERGUSSON, R.
Selected poems of Allan Ramsay and
Robert Fergusson. (*ed.* A. M. Kinghorn *and*
A. Law)
Scottish Academic Press, 1974.
Fergusson—a bi-centenary handsel.
(*ed.* R. Garioch)
Reprographia, 1974.

GARIOCH, R.
Selected poems.
Macdonald, 1966.
Doktor Faust in Rose Street.
*Macdonald, 1973.

HENRYSON, R.
Poems. (*ed.* C. Elliott) 2nd ed.
O.U.P., 1975.
Selected poems. (*ed.* D. Murison)
Saltire, 1952.
[Poems] selected by H. MacDiarmid.
*Penguin, 1973.

HOGG, J.
Selected poems. (*ed.* D. S. Mack)
O.U.P., 1971.

MacCAIG, N.
Selected poems.
Hogarth Press, 1971. (o.p.)
Akros No. 7.
Akros, 1968.
The white bird.
Hogarth Press, 1973.
The world's room.
Hogarth Press, 1974. (o.p.)

MacDIARMID, H.
The Hugh MacDiarmid anthology.
(*ed.* M. Grieve *and* A. Scott)
Routledge & Kegan Paul, 1972.
Selected poems. (*ed.* D. Craig *and* J. Manson)
*Penguin, 1970. (o.p.)
A drunk man looks at the thistle.
(*ed.* D. Daiches)
Caledonia Press, 1953. (o.p.)
Akros, Nos. 13 and 14.
Akros, 1970.

MACLEAN, S.
Poems to Eimhir, (*trans.* I. Crichton Smith).
Gollancz, 1971.
*Northern House, 1971.
*Lines Review*, No. 34, September, 1970.
*Macdonald.

MORGAN, E.
From Glasgow to Saturn.
*Carcanet Press, 1973.
Glasgow sonnets.
Castlelaw Press, 1973. (o.p.)
The horseman's word.
*Akros, 1970. (o.p.)
Instamatic poems.
McKelvie, 1972.
*in* Penguin modern poets, No. 15.
*Penguin, 1969. (o.p.)
The second life: selected poems.
*Edinburgh University Press, 1968.
The Whittrick.
*Akros, 1973.

MUIR, E.
Collected poems. (*ed.* Willa Muir *and*
J. C. Hall) 2nd ed.
Faber, 1963.
Selected poems.
*Faber, 1965.

RAMSAY, A.
Selected poems of Allan Ramsay and
Robert Fergusson. (*ed.* A. M. Kinghorn *and*
A. Law)
Scottish Academic Press, 1974.

SCOTT, *Sir* W.
Selected poems. (*ed.* T. Crawford)
*O.U.P., 1972.

SMITH, Iain Crichton
Hamlet in Autumn.
Macdonald, 1972.

Love poems and elegies.
Gollancz, 1972.
Selected poems.
Gollancz, 1970.

SMITH, Sydney Goodsir
Collected Poems: 1941–1975.
The Scottish Library.
John Calder, 1957.
*Akros*, 10, May 1969.
Kynd Kittock's Land.
*Macdonald, 1965.
Under the Eildon Tree. 2nd rev. ed.
Serif Books, 1954. (o.p.)

SOUTAR, W.
Collected poems. (*ed.* H. MacDiarmid)
Dakers, 1948. (o.p.)
Poems in Scots and English.
(*ed.* W. R. Aitken) (1961)
Scottish Academic Press, 1975.

STEVENSON, R. L.
Collected poems. (*ed.* J. A. Smith)
Hart-Davis, 1971.

## E. Other Twentieth-Century Poets of interest:

AITCHISON, J.
Sounds before sleep.
Chatto & Windus, 1971. (o.p.)

ANNAND, J. K.
Sing it aince for pleisure.
*Macdonald, 1965.
Twice for joy.
*Macdonald, 1973.
Two voices.
*Macdonald, 1968.

ANGUS, M.
Selected poems. (*ed.* M. Lindsay)
Serif Books, 1950. (o.p.)

BLACK, D. M.
*in* Penguin modern poets, No. 11.
*Penguin, 1968. (o.p.)

BOLD, A.
*in* Penguin modern poets, No. 15.
*Penguin, 1969. (o.p.)

BRUCE, G.
Collected poems.
Edinburgh University Press, 1970.

CAMPBELL, D.
Rhymes 'n reasons.
Reprographia, 1972.

COCKER, W. D.
Poems Scots and English.
Brown, Son & Ferguson, 1932. (o.p.)

CONN, S.
An ear to the ground.
*Hutchinson, 1972.

CORRIE, J.
The image o' God.
Faber, 1937. (o.p.)

COSTIE, C. M.
The collected Orkney dialect poems.
Kirkwall Press, 1974.

CRUIKSHANK, H. B.
Collected poems.
Reprographia, 1971.

DUNN, D.
Love or nothing.
Faber, 1975.

GARRY, F.
Bennygoak and other poems.
*Akros, 1974.

GRAHAM, W. S.
in Penguin modern poets, No. 17.
*Penguin, 1970.

GRAY, Sir A.
Selected poems. (ed. M. Lindsay)
Maclellan, 1948. (o.p.)

JACKSON, A.
in Penguin modern poets, No. 12.
*Penguin, 1969.

JACOB, V.
Scottish poems.
Oliver & Boyd, 1944. (o.p.)

LEE, J.
Ballads of battle.
Murray, 1917. (o.p.)

LEONARD, T.
Poems.
*O'Brien, 1973.

LINDSAY, M.
Selected poems, 1942–1972.
Robert Hale, 1973.

LOCHHEAD, L.
Memo for Spring.
*Reprographia, 1972.

MacBETH, G.
Collected poems 1958–1970.
*Macmillan, 1971.

MACKIE, A. D.
Clytach.
*Akros, 1972.

MACLEAN, Alasdair
From the wilderness.
*Gollancz, 1973.

MACLEAN, S; CAMPBELL HAY, G;
NEILL, W; MacGREGOR S.
Four points of a Saltire.
Reprographia, 1970. (o.p.)

MACLEOD, J.
An old olive tree.
Macdonald, 1971.

MILNE, J. C.
Poems.
Aberdeen University Press, 1963.

MUNRO, R.
Shetland, like the world.
Triangle Press, 1973.

MURRAY, C.
Hamewith, and other poems. (1927)
Constable, 1968.
Last poems.
Aberdeen University Press, 1969.

REID, A.
Passwords: places, poems and pre-occupations.
Weidenfeld & Nicolson, 1964. (o.p.)
Weathering: selected poems.
André Deutsch, 1975.

RORIE, D.
The lum hat wantin' the croon. (1935)
Chambers, 1965.

ROSS, Sandy Thomas
Bairnsangs.
Macmillan, 1957. (o.p.)

SCOTT, A.
Selected poems, 1943–1974.
Akros, 1975.

TREMAYNE, S.
Selected and new poems.
Chatto & Windus, 1973.

TURNER, W. P.
The moral rocking horse.
Barrie & Jenkins, 1970. (o.p.)

WINGATE, W.
Poems.
Gowans & Gray, 1919. (o.p.)

YOUNG, A.
Complete poems.
*Secker & Warburg, 1974.

YOUNG, D.
Selected poems.
Oliver & Boyd, 1950.

**F. Unclassifiable**

McGONAGALL, W.
A library omnibus.
Duckworth, 1969.
includes *Poetic gems (1934),
*More poetic gems (1966) and
*Last poetic gems (1968).

# Poetry: Critical Works

*Denotes a paperback edition.

**A. Critical and background material wholly or partly devoted to poetry:**

BUCHAN, D.
The ballad and the folk.
Routledge & Kegan Paul, 1972.

CRAIG, D.
Scottish literature and the Scottish people, 1680–1830.
Chatto & Windus, 1961.

EMMERSON, G. S.
A social history of Scottish dance.
McGill-Queen's University Press, 1972.

GLEN, D.
Hugh MacDiarmid and the Scottish Renaissance.
Chambers, 1964.

FULTON, R.
Contemporary Scottish poetry.
Macdonald, 1974.

HODGART, M.
The ballads.
Hutchinson, 1962. (o.p.)

KINSLEY, J. ed.
Scottish poetry, a critical survey.
Cassell, 1955. (o.p.)

MORGAN, E.
Essays.
Carcanet Press, 1974.

MUIR, E.
The estate of poetry.
Hogarth Press, 1962.

MUIR, W.
Living with ballads.
Hogarth Press, 1965.

REED, J.
Border ballads.
Athlone Press, 1973.

SMITH, S. G.
A short introduction to Scottish literature.
Serif Books, 1951. (o.p.)

THOMSON, D.
An introduction to Gaelic poetry.
Gollancz, 1974.

WITTIG, K.
The Scottish tradition in literature. (1958)
Greenwood Press, 1972.

**B. On Individual Poets**

BURNS:  Crawford, T.
Burns: a study of the poems and songs.
*Oliver & Boyd, 1960. (o.p.)

Daiches, D.
Robert Burns and his world.
Thames & Hudson, 1971.

Ferguson, J. de Lancey
Letters of Robert Burns.
O.U.P., 1931. (o.p.)

Lindsay, M.
The Burns encyclopedia.
(rev. ed.)
Hutchinson, 1970.

DUNBAR:  Scott, T.
Dunbar: a critical exposition of the poems.
Oliver & Boyd, 1966. (o.p.)

FERGUSSON:  Maclaine, A.
Robert Fergusson.
New York: Twayne, 1965.

Smith, S. G. ed.
Robert Fergusson 1750–1774, essays by various hands.
Nelson, 1952. (o.p.)

HENRYSON:    MacQueen, J.
Robert Henryson: a study of
the major narrative poems.
O.U.P., 1967.

MacDIARMID:    Buthlay, K.
Hugh MacDiarmid.
Oliver & Boyd, 1964. (o.p.)

Glen, D.
Hugh MacDiarmid and the
Scottish Renaissance.
Chambers, 1964.

Glen, D. *ed.*
Hugh MacDiarmid: a
critical survey.
Scottish Academic Press,
1972.

Smith, I. C.
The golden lyric.
Akros, 1967. (o.p.)

Akros, Nos. 13 and 14.
Akros, 1970.

MUIR:    Butter, P.
Edwin Muir.
*Oliver & Boyd, 1962. (o.p.)

Butter, P.
Edwin Muir: man and poet.
Oliver & Boyd, 1966. (o.p.)

Muir, Willa
Belonging: a memoir.
Hogarth Press, 1968.

RAMSEY:    Martin, Burns
Allan Ramsay: a study of
his life and works. (1931)
Greenwood Press, 1973.

STEVENSON:    Daiches, D.
R. L. Stevenson.
Maclellan, 1952.

Daiches, D.
Robert Louis Stevenson and
his world.
Thames & Hudson, 1973.

Furnas, J. C.
Voyage to windward: the
life of Robert Louis
Stevenson.
Faber, 1952. (o.p.)

# Children's Fiction with a Scottish Setting for the Secondary School

*Denotes a paperback edition.

ALLAN, Mabel Esther
A formidable enemy.
Heinemann, 1973.
Holiday of endurance.
Dent, 1961. (o.p.)
Island in a green sea.
Dent, 1973.
Stranger in Skye.
White Lion, 1974.

ARTHUR, Ruth Mabel
Autumn people.
Gollancz, 1973.

ARUNDEL, Honor
The blanket word.
H. Hamilton, 1973.
Emma in love.
H. Hamilton, 1970.
*Pan, 1973.
Emma's island.
H. Hamilton, 1968.
*Pan, 1972.
A family failing.
H. Hamilton, 1972.
The girl in the opposite bed.
H. Hamilton, 1970.
*Macmillan Education, 1972.
Green Street.
H. Hamilton, 1966.
The high house.
H. Hamilton, 1967.
*Pan, 1972.
The longest weekend.
H. Hamilton, 1969.
The terrible temptation.
H. Hamilton, 1971.
The two sisters.
Heinemann, 1968.

BATTEN, H. Mortimer
The singing forest.
Heinemann, 1960.

BAWDEN, Nina
The witch's daughter.
Gollancz, 1966.
Heinemann, 1972.
*Penguin, 1969.

BAYLEY, Viola
Scottish adventure.
Dent, 1965. (o.p.)

BEARDMORE, George
Islands of strangers.
Macdonald, 1968. (o.p.)

BELL, J. J.
Wee Macgreegor. (1902)
Chambers, 1933. (o.p.)

BOHAN, Edmund
The buckler.
Hutchinson, 1972.

BROSTER, D. K.
The dark mile. (1929)
Heinemann, 1962.
*Penguin, 1974.
The flight of the heron. (1925)
Heinemann, 1952.
*Penguin, 1971.
The gleam in the north. (1927)
Heinemann, 1952.
*Penguin, 1971.

CAMPBELL, Marion
Lances and longships.
Dent, 1963.
The squire of Val.
Dent, 1967.

The wide blue road.
Dent, 1967. (o.p.)
CARTER, P.
Madatan.
Oxford University Press, 1974.
CHIPPERFIELD, Joseph E.
Lone stands the glen.
Hutchinson, 1966 (o.p.)
The two fugitives.
Heinemann, 1966.
Wolf of Badenoch.
Hutchinson, 1958. (o.p.)
CURRY, Jane Louise
The sleepers.
Dobson, 1969.
CUTT, W. Towrie
Carry my bones northwest.
André Deutsch, 1973.
Message from Arkmae.
André Deutsch, 1972.
Seven for the sea.
André Deutsch, 1972.
DERWENT, Lavinia
The boy from Sula.
Gollancz, 1973.
Return to Sula.
Gollancz, 1971.
*Pan, 1974.
Sula.
Gollancz, 1969.
*Pan, 1974.
DUNCAN, Jane
Camerons ahoy!
Macmillan, 1968.
Camerons at the castle.
Macmillan, 1964.
Camerons calling.
Macmillan, 1966.
Camerons on the hills.
Macmillan, 1963.
*Brockhampton, 1967.
Camerons on the train.
Macmillan, 1963.
My friends the Miss Boyds.
Macmillan, 1959.
EASTON, Stephen
Gentle Jackson.
Macmillan, 1970.
FIDLER, Kathleen
The boy with the bronze axe.
Oliver & Boyd, 1968.
*Penguin, 1972.
Flash, the sheep dog.
Lutterworth Press, 1965. (o.p.)
Haki, the shetland pony. (1968)
*Brockhampton, 1973.
Mountain rescue dog.
Lutterworth Press, 1969.
FINLAY, Campbell
Farewell to the Western Isles.
Harrap, 1964.

Fisherman's gold.
Harrap, 1960. (o.p.)
FINLAY, Winifred
Beadbonny ash.
Harrap, 1973.
The singing stones.
Harrap, 1970.
Summer of the golden stag.
Harrap, 1969.
HARRIS, Rosemary
The seal-singing.
Faber, 1971.
HOLDEN, Molly
Reiver's weather.
Chatto, 1973.
HUNTER, Mollie
The bodach.
Blackie, 1970.
The ferlie.
Blackie, 1968.
The ghosts of Glencoe.
Evans, 1966. (o.p.)
The haunted mountain.
H. Hamilton, 1972.
Hi Johnny.
Evans, 1963. (o.p.)
The kelpie's pearls.
*Penguin, 1973.
The Lothian run.
H. Hamilton, 1971.
*Penguin, 1974.
A pistol in Greenyards.
Evans, 1965. (o.p.)
The sound of chariots.
H. Hamilton, 1973.
The Spanish letters.
*Penguin, 1972.
The stronghold.
H. Hamilton, 1974.
The thirteenth member.
H. Hamilton, 1971.
Thomas and the warlock.
Blackie, 1967. (o.p.)
JACKSON, Rosemary Elizabeth
Aunt Eleanor.
Chatto, 1969.
The poltergeist.
Chatto, 1968.
The wheel of the Finfolk.
Chatto, 1972.
KELLAM, Ian
The first summer year.
O.U.P., 1972.
KISSELL, George
The sword of McAra.
Angus & Robertson, 1968. (o.p.)
KYLE, Elisabeth
Girl with a lantern: Grizel Hume.
Evans, 1961.
The house of the pelican.
Nelson, 1954. (o.p.)

LEA, Alec
Temba dawn.
Bodley Head, 1974.

LINGARD, Joan
Clearance.
H. Hamilton, 1974.

LYON, Elinor
Strangers at the door.
Brockhampton Press, 1967. (o.p.)

MacALPINE, Margaret
Anra, the storm child.
Faber, 1965. (o.p.)
The black gull of Corrie Lechan.
Faber, 1964. (o.p.)

McFARLANE, Iris
The summer of the lame seagull.
Chatto, Boyd & Oliver, 1970.

McGREGOR, Iona
The burning hill.
Faber, 1970.
An Edinburgh reel.
Faber, 1968.
The popinjay.
Faber, 1969.
The tree of liberty.
Faber, 1972.

McKELLAR, William
Davie's wee dog.
Bodley Head.
A dog like no other.
Wheaton, 1967.
A very small miracle.
Macdonald, 1970.

McLEAN, Allan Campbell
The hill of the red fox. (1955)
Collins, 1968.
*Collins, 1973.
Master of Morgana. (1960)
*Collins, 1974.
Ribbon of fire. (1962)
*Penguin, 1968.
(in Gaelic) Gairm Publications, 1967.
A sound of trumpets. (1967)
Collins, 1971.
Storm over Skye.
Collins, 1968.
(originally published as 'The man of the house' (1956))
The year of the stranger. (1971)
*Collins, 1973.

MacPHERSON, Margaret
The battle of the braes.
Collins, 1972. (o.p.)
The boy on the roof.
Collins, 1974.
The new tenants.
Collins, 1968. (o.p.)
The rough road.
Collins, 1968. (o.p.)
The shinty boys.
Collins, 1968. (o.p.)

MAKIN, Irene
Wild cat.
Hutchinson, 1968.

MITCHISON, Naomi
The big house. (1950)
Birmingham: Combridge, 1970.
The far harbour.
Collins, 1969.
The land the ravens found.
Collins, 1955. (o.p.)

OLIVER, Jane
Charlie is my darling.
Chatto, Boyd & Oliver, 1969.
Queen most fair.
Macmillan, 1959.

POLLAND, Madeleine
The queen's blessing.
Longman, 1964.
Stranger in the hills.
Hutchinson, 1969.
To kill a king.
Hutchinson, 1970.

RANSOME, A.
Great Northern.
Cape, 1947.
*Penguin, 1971.

RUNDLE, Anne
Dragonscale.
Hutchinson, 1969.
Tamlane.
Hutchinson, 1970.

RUTHIN, Margaret
Secret of the Shetlands.
Dobson, 1963. (o.p.)

STEPHEN, David
Rory the roebuck.
Bodley Head, 1961. (o.p.)
String Lug the fox.
Lutterworth, 1950. (o.p.)
(abridged) Collins, 1961. (o.p.)

STEWART, Agnes Charlotte
Falcon's crag.
Blackie, 1969.

STEWART, Mary
Wildfire at midnight.
Hodder, 1956.
*Hodder, 1968.

STRANGER, Joyce
Paddy Joe.
Collins, 1971.
Rusty.
Harvill Press, 1969.
*Transworld, 1971.
Secret herds and other animal stories.
Dent, 1974.
Trouble for Paddy Joe.
Collins, 1973.

SUDBERY, Rodie
Curious place.
André Deutsch, 1973.

SUTCLIFF, Rosemary
The mark of the horse lord.
O.U.P., 1965.

TARN, William Woodthorpe
The treasure of the isle of mist. (1919)
O.U.P., 1959.

TRANTER, Nigel
Border riding.
Brockhampton, 1958. (o.p.)
Fire and high water.
Collins, 1967. (o.p.)

Something very fishy.
Collins, 1962. (o.p.)
Tinker Tess.
Dobson, 1967.

WILLARD, Barbara
Battle of Wednesday week.
Longman, 1963.
*Penguin, 1968.

# A Selection of Non-Fiction

## 1. Out of Doors

*Denotes a paperback edition.

ALLAN, J. R.
North-east lowlands of Scotland. (rev. ed.)
Robert Hale, 1974.

BLAKE, George
The Firth of Clyde.
Collins, 1952. (o.p.)

BORTHWICK, Alastair
Always a little further. (1939)
Smith, 1969.

BROWN, Ivor
Balmoral.
Collins, 1966. (o.p.)

BROWN, P. Hume
Early travellers in Scotland. (1891)
Mercat Press, 1973.

COOPER, Derek
Skye.
Routledge & Kegan Paul, 1970.

DARLING, F. Fraser
Island years. (1940)
*Pan, 1973.
A naturalist on Rona.
O.U.P., 1939. (o.p.)

DARLING, F. Fraser and BOYD, J. Morton
The Highland and Islands.
Collins, 1969.
*Fontana, 1969.

DOUGLAS, Hugh
Portrait of the Burns country. (2nd ed.)
Robert Hale, 1973.

FRASER, Duncan
East coast oil town.
Montrose Standard Press, 1975.

GORDON, Seton
Highland days.
Cassell, 1968. (o.p.)
Highland summer.
Cassell, 1971.

GRAHAM, Cuthbert
Portrait of Aberdeen and Deeside.
Robert Hale, 1972.

GUNN, Neil M.
Highland Pack.
Faber, 1949. (o.p.)

HOUSE, Jack
The heart of Glasgow. (rev. ed.)
Hutchinson, 1972.

KEITH, Alexander
A thousand years of Aberdeen.
Aberdeen University Press, 1972.

LINDSAY, Maurice
By yon bonnie banks: a gallimaufry.
Hutchinson, 1961. (o.p.)

LINKLATER, Eric
Orkney and Shetland. (rev. ed.)
Robert Hale, 1971.

LOCHHEAD, Marion
Portrait of the Scott country. (2nd. ed.)
Robert Hale, 1973.

McLEAN, Allan Campbell
Explore the Highlands and Islands. (2nd. ed.)
*H.I.D.B., 1973.

MACLEAN, Calum
The Highlands.
Batsford, 1957. (o.p.)

MACLEAN, Charles
Island on the edge of the world: Utopian
St. Kilda and its passing.
Stacey, 1972.

MAXWELL, Gavin
Harpoon at a venture.
*New English Library, 1972. (o.p.)

MONCRIEFF, G. Scott
The lowlands of Scotland.
Batsford, 1939. (o.p.)

MURRAY, W. H.
Highland landscape.
National Trust for Scotland, 1962.
Mountaineering in Scotland. (rev. ed.)
Dent, 1962.

NETHERSOLE-THOMPSON, Desmond,
*and* WATSON, Adam
The Cairngorms: their natural history
and scenery.
Collins, 1974.

OAKLEY, Charles
'The second city.' (3rd ed.)
Blackie, 1975.

REID, J. M.
Glasgow,
Batsford, 1956. (o.p.)

SELBY, John
Over the sea to Skye.
H. Hamilton, 1973.

SIMPSON, W. Douglas
Portrait of Skye and the Outer Hebrides.
Robert Hale, 1973.
Portrait of the Highlands.
Robert Hale, 1972.

SCOTTISH MOUNTAINEERING CLUB
District guide books. 9v.
Reading: West Col Productions for the
Scottish Mountaineering Trust. (frequently
revised; current editions 1971-5)

TRANTER, Nigel
The eastern counties.
Hodder, 1972.
The heartland of Scotland.
Hodder, 1971.
Portrait of the Border country.
Robert Hale, 1972.

WHITE, John Talbot, *ed.*
The Scottish border and Northumberland.
*Eyre Methuen, 1973.

WYNESS, Fenton
City by the grey north sea: Aberdeen.
Impulse Books, 1972.

YOUNGSON, A. J. *ed.*
Beyond the Highland line.
Collins, 1974.

# 2. Biography and Autobiography

*Denotes a paperback edition.

ALLAN, J. R.
Farmer's boy. (1935) (*ed.* D. M. Budge)
Longman, 1974.

BOSWELL, James
Journal of a tour to the Hebrides. (1785)
*O.U.P., 1970. (Hardback also)
(*ed.* R. W. Chapman) (1924)

BRIDIE, James
One way of living.
Constable, 1939. (o.p.)

BUCHAN, John
Montrose.
Nelson, 1928. (o.p.)

CAMPBELL, Ian M.
Thomas Carlyle.
H. Hamilton, 1974.

CARLYLE, Thomas
Reminiscences. (1881–7)
Dent, 1972.

CASKIE, Donald
The tartan pimpernel. (1957)
*Fontana, 1960.

COCKBURN, Henry
Memorials of his time. (1856)
Mercat Press, 1971.

COWAN, Evelyn
Spring remembered: a Scottish Jewish
childhood.
*Southside, 1974.

DAICHES, David
Charles Edward Stuart: life and times
of Bonnie Prince Charlie.
Thames & Hudson, 1973.
*Pan, 1975.
Two worlds.
Macmillan, 1957. (o.p.)

DUFF, David
Victoria in the Highlands.
Muller, 1968.

FRASER, Amy S.
The hills of home.
Routledge & Kegan Paul, 1973.

GRANT, Elizabeth
Memoirs of a Highland lady. (1898; rev. ed.
1950)
Murray, 1967.

GUNN, Neil Miller
The atom of delight.
Faber, 1956. (o.p.)

HAMILTON, Iain
Scotland the brave.
Michael Joseph, 1957. (o.p.)

HANLEY, Clifford
Dancing in the streets. (1958)
*U. R. Books, 1972.

HAYNES, Dorothy K.
Haste ye back.
Jarrolds, 1973.

HENDRY, J. F.
Fernie Brae: a Scottish childhood.
Maclellan, 1947.

MacDIARMID, Hugh
The company I've kept.
Hutchinson, 1966. (o.p.)
Lucky poet. (1943)
Cape, 1972.
Scottish eccentrics. (1936)
Johnson Reprint Corporation, 1972.

McLELLAN, Angus
The furrow behind me.
Routledge, 1962. (o.p.)

MAXWELL, Gavin
The house of Elrig.
Longman, 1965. (o.p.)

MILLER, Hugh
My schools and schoolmasters. (1854)
Morton, 1905. (o.p.)

MILLER, Karl, *ed.*
Memoirs of a modern Scotland.
Faber, 1970.

MUIR, Edwin
An autobiography. (1954)
Hogarth Press, 1965.
*Methuen, 1965.

NIALL, Iain
A Galloway childhood.
Heinemann, 1967.

RAMSAY, Dean
Reminiscences of Scottish life and
character. (enlarged edition 1874)
(abridged) Robert Grant, 1947. (o.p.)

REA, F. G.
A school in South Uist, 1890–1913.
Routledge & Kegan Paul, 1964. (o.p.)

REID, J. M.
James Lithgow, Master of Work.
Hutchinson, 1964. (o.p.)

SCOTT, Alexander
Still life: William Soutar.
Chambers, 1958. (o.p.)

SILLAR, Eleanor
Edinburgh's child.
Oliver & Boyd, 1961. (o.p.)

STEVENSON, Robert Louis
Across the plains.
Chatto & Windus, 1892. (o.p.)

The amateur emigrant. (1895)
Chatto & Windus, 1910. (o.p.)
Memories and portraits. (1887)
Heinemann, 1925. (o.p.)
The Silverado squatters.
Chatto & Windus, 1883. (o.p.)
Travels with a donkey.
Longman, 1964.

SUTHERLAND, Donald
Butt and ben: a Highland boyhood.
Blackwood, 1963.

VICTORIA, Queen
Our life in the Highlands.
Kimber, 1968.

WATERSON, Charles
Hugh Miller, the Cromarty stonemason.
*National Trust for Scotland, 1961.

WEIR, Molly
Best foot forward.
Hutchinson, 1972.
*Pan, 1974.
Shoes were for Sunday.
Hutchinson, 1970.
*Pan, 1973.
A toe on the ladder.
Hutchinson, 1973.
*Pan, 1975.

# 3. Stories and Legends

*Denotes a paperback edition.

AITKEN, Hannah, *ed.*
A forgotten heritage: original folk tales
of Lowland Scotland.
Scottish Academic Press, 1973.

BROWN, George Mackay
The two fiddlers.
Chatto & Windus, 1974.

FINLAY, Winifred
Folk tales from moor and mountain.
Kaye and Ward, 1969.

JACOBS, J., *ed.*
Celtic fairy tales. (1892)
Bodley Head, 1970.
*Dover, 1968.

LANG, Andrew
The gold of Fairnilee
and other stories. (*ed.* G. Avery)
Gollancz, 1967.

LEODHAS, Sorche Nic
Claymore and kilt.
Bodley Head, 1971. (o.p.)
Gaelic ghosts.
Bodley Head, 1966.
Scottish ghosts. (new ed. of *Gaelic ghosts*)
*Pan, 1974.
Thistle and thyme.
Bodley Head, 1975.
Twelve great black cats.
Bodley Head, 1972.

LYFORD-PIKE, M.
Scottish fairy tales.
Dent, 1974.

MACDOUGALL, Carl
A cuckoo's nest.
Molendinar Press, 1974.

MACFARLANE, Iris
The mouth of the night: Gaelic stories retold.
Chatto & Windus, 1973.

McNEILL, F. Marian
Hallowe'en.
Albyn Press, 1970.
The silver bough. 4 vols.
Maclellan, 1957–70.

MONTGOMERIE, Nora *and* William
The well at the world's end.
Bodley Head, 1975.

PICARD, Barbara Leonie, *ed.*
Hero tales from the British Isles.
*Penguin.

SANDERS, Ruth Manning
Stories from the English and Scottish
ballads.
Heinemann, 1968.

SCOTT, H. *and* SCOTT, T. *eds.*
True Thomas the Rhymer, and other
tales of the Lowland Scots.
O.U.P., 1971.

SCOTT, Tom, *ed.*
Tales of King Robert the Bruce.
Pergamon, 1969. (o.p.)
Reprographia, 1975.

SUTCLIFF, Rosemary
The high deeds of Finn MacCool.
Bodley Head, 1967.
*Penguin, 1968.

SWIRE, Otta F.
The Highlands and their legends.
Oliver & Boyd, 1963. (o.p.)
The Outer Hebrides and their legends.
Oliver & Boyd, 1966.
Skye: the island and its legends.
Blackie, 1973.

WILSON, Barbara Ker, *ed.*
Scottish folk tales and legends.
O.U.P., 1954.

WOOD, W.
Legends of the borders.
Impulse Books, 1973.

WYNESS, Fenton
Legends of north-east Scotland.
*Impulse Books, 1972.

**Periodical**
TOCHER: tales, songs, traditions selected from
the archives of the School of Scottish Studies.
Quarterly.
School of Scottish Studies, University
of Edinburgh.

# 4. Picture Books

*Denotes a paperback edition.

BLAKE, George *and others*
Scotland's splendour.
Collins, 1960. (rev. ed. 1971)

BUTT, DONNACHIE *and* HUME
Glasgow.
David & Charles, 1968. (o.p.)
Industrial history in pictures: Scotland.
David & Charles, 1968. (o.p.)

DUNNETT, Alastair Inglis
Scotland in colour.
Batsford, 1970.

DUNNETT, Alastair M., *ed.*
Alistair Maclean introduces Scotland.
André Deutsch, 1972.

FITZGIBBON, Theodora
A taste of Scotland in food and pictures.
Dent, 1970.
*Pan, 1971.

HOUSE, Jack
The glory of Scotland.
Vol. 1: The West.
Oliver & Boyd, 1962. (o.p.)
Vol. 2: The East.
Chambers, 1965. (o.p.)

HUME, John R.
Industrial archaeology of Glasgow.
Blackie, 1974.

LINKLATER, Eric *and* SMITH, Edwin
Scotland.
Thames & Hudson, 1968. (o.p.)

MINTO, C. S.
Victorian and Edwardian Edinburgh from
old photographs.
Batsford, 1973.
Victorian and Edwardian Scotland from
old photographs.
Batsford, 1970.

STEPHEN, David
Scottish wild life.
Hutchinson, 1964. (o.p.)

TAYLOR, Wilfred
Scotland in colour.
Batsford, 1973.

URQUHART, G. *and* MARLIN ,W.
Dumfries and Galloway: our story in pictures.
Dumfries: Sangspiel, 1972.

# 5. Animal Books

*Denotes a paperback edition.

DARLING, F. Fraser.
A herd of red deer.
O.U.P., 1937. (o.p.)

FARRE, Rowena
Seal morning.
Hutchinson, 1960.
*Arrow books, 1970. (o.p.)

GORDON, Seton
The golden eagle.
Collins, 1955. (o.p.)

MacNALLY, Lea
Highland year. (1968)
*Pan, 1972.
Wild Highlands.
Dent, 1972.
The year of the red deer.
Dent, 1975.

MAXWELL, Gavin
The otter's tale.
Longman, 1962.
*Pan, 1971.

Ring of bright water.
Longman, 1960.
*Pan, 1969.

NETHERSOLE-THOMPSON, D.
Highland birds.
*H.I.D.B., 1971.

PERRY, Richard
The watcher and the red deer.
David & Charles, 1971.

STEPHEN, David
Highland animals.
*Collins, 1974.
Guide to watching wild life.
*Collins, 1973.

WATERSTON, G. and DENNIS, R.
Ospreys and Speyside wildlife.
*R.S.P.B., 1973.

# 6. Popular History

*Denotes a paperback edition.   †Denotes availability for younger readers.

BARCLAY, J. B.
Edinburgh.
Black, 1965. (o.p.)

BROWN, George Mackay
An Orkney tapestry.
Gollancz, 1969.
*Quartet Books, 1973.

CAMERON, A. D.
Living in Scotland, 1760–1820.
*Oliver & Boyd, 1969.

CRUDEN, Stuart
The Scottish castle.
Nelson, 1960. (o.p.)

DONALDSON, Gordon
Scotland: the shaping of a nation.
David & Charles, 1974.

DONALDSON, G. and MORPETH, R. S.
Who's who in Scottish history.
Blackwell, 1974.

ELDER, Madge
Ballad country.
Oliver & Boyd, 1963. (o.p.)

FRASER, George MacDonald
The steel bonnets.
Barrie & Jenkins, 1971.
*Pan, 1974.

GLOVER, Janet R.
The story of Scotland.
Faber, 1960.
*Faber, 1966.

GRIMBLE, Ian
The trial of Patrick Sellar.
Routledge & Kegan Paul, 1962. (o.p.)

HALDANE, A. R. B.
The drove roads of Scotland. (1950)
David & Charles, 1973.
New ways through the glens. (1962)
David & Charles, 1973.

HAYMAN, Sylvia
†Bonnie Prince Charlie.
Macdonald.

INNES of LEARNEY, Sir Thomas
The tartans of the clans and families
of Scotland. (8th rev. ed.)
Johnston & Bacon, 1971.

KELLETT, J. R.
Glasgow.
Blond Educational, 1967.

LINKLATER, Eric
The prince in the heather.
Hodder, 1965.

LOBBAN, R. D.
†The clansmen.
U.L.P., 1970.

MacKENZIE, Agnes Mure
Scottish pageant. 4v.
Oliver & Boyd, 1946–50. (o.p.)

MacKENZIE, Osgood H.
A hundred years in the Highlands. (1921)
Geoffrey Bles, 1972.

MACKIE, J. D.
A history of Scotland.
*Penguin, 1970.

McLAREN, Moray
The wisdom of the Scots.
Michael Joseph, 1961. (o.p.)

MacLEAN, Sir Fitzroy
A concise history of Scotland.
Thames & Hudson, 1970.

MacPHAIL, I. M. M.
A history of Scotland, books 1 & 2.
Edward Arnold, 1956.

MAXWELL, David
Bygone Scotland. (1894)
S. R. Publishers, 1970.

MAXWELL, *Sir* John Stirling
Shrines and homes of Scotland. (1937)
Chambers, 1958.

MILLER, Margaret J.
†King Robert the Bruce.
Macdonald.

MITCHISON, Rosalind
A history of Scotland.
Methuen, 1970.
*Methuen, 1970.

NICHOL, Norman
Glasgow: from the earliest times
to the present day.
Black, 1970.

PREBBLE, John
Culloden.
Secker & Warburg, 1961.
*Penguin, 1970.
The high girders.
Secker & Warburg, 1975.
*Pan, 1968.
The Highland clearances.
Secker & Warburg, 1963.
*Penguin, 1969.
The lion in the North.
Secker & Warburg, 1971.
*Penguin, 1973.

ROLT, Lionel T. C.
Red for danger.
David & Charles, 1971.
*Pan, 1971.

SMOUT, T. C.
A history of the Scottish People 1560–1830.
Collins, 1969.
*Fontana, 1972.

STEVENSON, Robert Louis
Edinburgh: Picturesque Notes.
Seeley & Co., 1879. (o.p.)

TRANTER, Nigel
The fortified house in Scotland. 5 vols.
Chambers, 1962–70.
†Outlaw of the Highlands: Rob Roy.
Dobson, 1965.

WATSON, Godfrey
The Border reivers.
Robert Hale, 1974.

## Then and There series: Longman

The Romans in Scotland, O. Thompson, 1968.
Scotland in the time of Wallace and Bruce,
W. K. Ritchie, 1970.
The days of James IV of Scotland, W. Stevenson,
1964.
Scotland in the days of James VI, Hyman
Shapiro, 1970.
The Jacobite Rising of 1745, William Stevenson,
1968.
Glasgow and the Tobacco Lords, Norman
Nichol, 1967.
Scotland in the days of Burns, Hyman Shapiro,
1968.
A Border woollen town in the Industrial
Revolution, Karen McKechnie, 1968.
Edinburgh in its Golden Age, W. K. Ritchie,
1967.
Glasgow in the Tramway Age, Ronald Brash,
1971.

Individual guides to properties in the care of
the National Trust for Scotland, and the ancient
monuments in the ownership or guardianship of
the Department of the Environment.

H

# Scottish Literary Periodicals

AKROS*
Akros Publications,
14 Parklands Avenue,
Penwortham, Preston, Lancs.
PR1 0QL

CHAPMAN*
W. Perrie, 118 Brankholm Brae,
Hamilton.

GAIRM*
Gairm Publications.
29 Waterloo Street,
GLASGOW.

GLASGOW REVIEW
J. Mulholland (ed.),
19–23 Dowanside Lane, Byres Road,
Glasgow, G12.

LALLANS
Lallans Society,
174 Craigleith Road,
Edinburgh.

LINES REVIEW*
Macdonald Publishers,
Edgefield Road,
Loanhead, Midlothian.

NEW EDINBURGH REVIEW*
Edinburgh University Student Publications,

1 Buccleuch Place,
Edinburgh, EH8 9LW

SCOTIA REVIEW*
D. Morrison (Editor),
33a Huddart Street,
Wick, Caithness.

SCOTTISH LITERARY JOURNAL
Association for Scottish Literary Studies,
Department of English,
Aberdeen University.

SCOTTISH LITERARY NEWS
Association for Scottish Literary Studies,
Department of English,
Aberdeen University.

SCOTTISH STUDIES
School of Scottish Studies,
Edinburgh University.

STUDIES IN SCOTTISH LITERATURE
Department of English,
University of South Carolina,
Columbia SC29208.
(5 Dollars for 4 issues)

TOCHER*
School of Scottish Studies,
Edinburgh University.

*Available from Scottish Association of Magazine Publishers, (S.C.A.M.P.) 55 Marchmont Road,
Edinburgh, EH9 1HT.

# Films, Video Tapes and Poetry Posters

## Films

1. *EDUCATIONAL FILMS OF SCOTLAND* (from S.C.F.L., 16–17 Woodside Terrace, Glasgow, G3 7XN)
   - (a) Cartoon: Holy Willie's prayer.                5 mins. DB71
   - (b) Cartoon: Sir Patrick Spens.                   8 mins. D1686
   - (c) Cartoon: Tam O'Shanter.                       11 mins. D1387
   - (d) Paintings: Tam O'Shanter.                     11 mins. DC3761
   - (e) Interview with Hugh MacDiarmid.
     (George Bruce interviews)                         15 mins. 2DC3584

2. *AMATEUR FILMS* (obtainable from EDUCATIONAL FILMS OF SCOTLAND)
   - (a) Cartoon: Ballad of young waters.              5 mins. DB76
   - (b) R. L. S. & Edinburgh: The grey metropolis.    15 mins. 2D1174

3. *FILMS OF SCOTLAND* (from Film House, 3 Randolph Crescent, Edinburgh EH3 7TJ)

   - (a) Hugh MacDiarmid: No fellow travellers.        25 mins.
   - (b) The practical romantic: Sir Walter Scott.     $23\frac{1}{2}$ mins.
   - (c) Sisyphus. (Cartoon of Garioch poem)           3 mins.
   - (d) A song for Prince Charlie. (A story of the '45 Stuart Rising.)                                         18 mins.
   - (e) Sorley Maclean's Island.                      23 mins.
   - (f) Grierson: Seawards the Great Ships.           30 mins.

4. *SCOTTISH FILM COUNCIL*, 16–17 Woodside Terrace, Glasgow, G3 7XN
   - (a) Neil Gunn.                                    20 mins.

5. *CONNOISSEUR FILMS, LONDON*, 167 Oxford Street, London, W1R 2DX
   (a) My childhood: Bill Douglas.                          48 mins.
   (b) My ain folk: Bill Douglas.                           60 mins.

6. *CENTRAL FILM LIBRARY*, Government Building, Bromyard Avenue, Acton, London, W3 7JB
   (a) Grierson: Drifters. (UK 58).                         50 mins.
   (b) Grierson: Seawards the Great Ships. (UK 1642).       30 mins.
   (c) Home and Away. (UK 1737).                            23 mins.

## Video Tapes

1. HUGH MacDIARMID: INTERVIEW
   IVC 961, produced by Aberdeen University Television for the Department of English; colour, 16 mins. (1″ tape)

2. HUGH MacDIARMID: POETRY
   As above, 19 mins.

3. THE THREE ESTATES
   Ampex 7003 (1″ tape), produced by Department of Drama, Glasgow University; 2 hours 36 mins.

## Poetry Posters

*Midnag Publications, Ashington, Northumberland.*

1. No. 20    Camas Tuath.            Tom Buchan
2. No. 21    The bonnie broukit bairn.   Hugh MacDiarmid
3. No. 24    Door of water.          George Mackay Brown
4. No. 25    Reothairt.              Sorley Maclean
5. No. 8     Sunset ploughing.       Norman MacCaig

# Records and Cassettes

## Argo
*117b, Fulham Road, London, SW3*
1. The poet speaks, volume nine. MacDiarmid/Goodsir Smith/ MacCaig/Crichton Smith. — PLP1089
2. The big hewer. Ewan MacColl & Charles Parker. — DA 140
3. Singing the fishing. Ewan MacColl & Charles Parker. — DA 142

## Claddagh
*Dame Street, Dublin*
1. A drunk man looks at the thistle. Read by Hugh MacDiarmid. — CCA 1–2
2. Barran agus asbhuain. Poems by Sorley MacLean read by himself. — CCA 3
3. The way I say it. Poems by N. MacCaig read by himself. — CCA 4
4. Hugh MacDiarmid. Reading his own poetry. — CCT 5
5. A double Scotch. Edwin Morgan and Alexander Scott reading their own poetry. — CCA 5

## Columbia
*20 Manchester Square, London, W1*
An evening with Robert Burns. Saltire Music Group. — 33CX 1317

## Ember Records (International) Ltd.
*Suite 4, Carlton Tower Place, Sloane Street, London, SW1*
Heather and Glen (Scots & Gaelic folk songs).
Alan Lomax and Hamish Henderson.

## Lallans Society

*13 Ashton Road, Glasgow, G12 8SP*

| | | |
|---|---|---|
| 1. An Edinburgh calendar. | ⎰ Cassettes of Robert Fergusson's | 001 |
| 2. People and places. | ⎱ poetry with commentary by Douglas | 006 |
| 3. The farmer's ingle and other poems. | Gifford. | 007 |

## Scottish Records

*Solsgirth, Kirkintilloch, Glasgow, G66 3XN*

A Scots song recital (settings of Burns and MacDiarmid) by
F. G. Scott            33 SR1 32

## Sounds Scotland

*Park Film Studios, Solsgirth, Kirkintilloch, Glasgow, G66 3XN*

| | |
|---|---|
| 1. Highland voyage. | LP 33 SR 120 / Cass. SRCM 120 |
| 2. The real Macrae. | LP 33 SR 123 / Cass. SRCM 123 |
| 3. Tam O'Shanter and other poems. Harold Wightman. | LP 33 SR 124 / Cass. SRC 124 |
| 4. More Burns poems. Tom Fleming. | Cass. SRC 125 |
| 5. The Scottish Renaissance poems 1922/1966. | Cass. SRC 127 |
| 6. The great McGonagall. Tom Fleming. | Cass. SRC 126 |
| 7. 'The Wee Cock Sparra and sic-like craturs'. Duncan Macrae. | EP SR 4517 / Cass. SRCS 101 |
| 8. Scottish songs—country style. Folk songs of N.E. Scotland. John Mearns. | Cass. SRCS 100 |
| 9. John Mearns sings Scottish folk songs. | EP SR 4512 |
| 10. Sang schule, Aberdeen. | LP 33 SR 134 |
| 11. The seventeenth century—music of castle, burgh and countryside. | SRSS 3 |
| 12. The eighteenth century—baroque and classical Scotland. | SRSS 4 |

## Tangent

*(West End Recordings Ltd.), 176a Holland Road, London, W14*

| | |
|---|---|
| 1. Traditional songs. Isla St. Clair. | TGS 112 |
| 2. Music from the Western Isles. | TNGM 110 |
| 3. Wauking songs from Barra. | TNGM 111 |
| 4. Scottish tradition no. 5: The muckle sangs: classic Scots ballads. | TNGM 119/D |
| 5. Scottish tradition no. 1: Bothy ballads. | TNGM 109 |

**Topic**

*27 Nassington Road, London, NW3 2TX*

1. Streets of song. Ewan MacColl & Dominic Behan.     12 T 41

2. The Jacobite Rebellions. (Songs of 1715 and 1745). Ewan MacColl & P. Seeger.     12 T 49

3. Princess of the thistle: Scots songs & ballads. Lizzie Higgins.     12 T 185

4. Scots songs & ballads. Norman Kennedy.     12 T 178

5. Steam whistle ballads. Ewan MacColl & Peggy Seeger.     12 T 104

6. Scottish songs. Jeannie Robertson.     12 T 96

7. The shepherd's song. Border ballads. Willie Scott.     12 T 183

8. Vagrant songs of Scotland. Isabel Sutherland.     12 T 151

9. The Child ballads I.     12 T 160

10. The Child ballads II.     12 T 161

11. Songs & ballads from the Lowland East of Scotland. Back o' Benachie.     12 T 180

12. The streets of Glasgow.     12 T S226

13. The Stewarts of Blair.     12 T 138

14. The travelling Stewarts.     12 T 179

15. Wild rover no more. Jimmy McBeath.     12 T 173

*Jeannie Robertson*
The Gallowa hills      COLLECTOR JES 1
The twa brothers      COLLECTOR JES 4
I ken where I'm going      COLLECTOR JES 8
Lord Donald      COLLECTOR JFS 4001
Jeannie's merry muse      HMV 7 EG 8534
Great traditional singers no. 1      TOPIC 12 T 96
The cuckoo's nest      PRESTIGE/INTERNATIONAL 13075
Jeannie Robertson      PRESTIGE/INTERNATIONAL 13006

*Jimmy MacBeath*
Come a' ye tramps and hawkers      COLLECTOR JES 10
Wild rover no more      TOPIC 12 T 173

*Jean Redpath*
Scottish ballad book      ELEKTRA EKL 214
Love, lilt and laughter      ELEKTRA EKL 224

*Lucy Stewart*
Child ballads      FOLKWAYS FG 3519
Glasgow street songs, vols. 1 & 2      COLLECTOR JES 2 & 5

*Ewan MacColl* (acc. Peggy Seeger)
Bothy ballads of Scotland      FOLKWAYS FW 8759

*Betsy Miller and Ewan MacColl*
A garland of Scots folksong      FOLK LYRIC FL 16

*Other recordings*
Columbia albums of old and
primitive music, vol. 6 (Scotland)      SL/209
Heather and glen      TRADITION TLP 1047
The Stewarts of Blair      TOPIC 12 T 138
The travelling Stewarts      TOPIC 12 T 179
Back o' Benachie      TOPIC 12 T 180
Festival at Blairgowrie      TOPIC 12 T 151
Songs of courtship      TOPIC 12 T 157
Songs of seduction      TOPIC 12 T 158

| | | |
|---|---|---|
| The Berryfields o' Blair | | PRESTIGE/INTERNATIONAL INT 25016 |
| The singing Campbells | | TOPIC 12 T 120 |
| *Pipe music* | | |
| John Burgess (Pibroch and Ceol Beag) | | FOLK LYRIC FL 112 |
| *Miscellaneous* | | |
| The Clutha | Scotia! | ARGO ZFB 18 |
| Willie Scott and others | The Borders | FOLKWAYS FW 8776 |
| A. L. Lloyd and Ewan MacColl | English & Scottish folk ballads | TOPIC 12 T 103 |
| Ewan MacColl | Chorus for the gallows | TOPIC 12 T 16 |
| Jeannie Robertson | Jeannie Robertson | TOPIC 12 T 96 |
| Willie Scott | The Shepherd's song, border ballads | TOPIC 12 T 183 |
| Hedy West | Old times & hard times | TOPIC 12 T 117 |
| Hedy West | Ballads | TOPIC 12 T 163 |
| The Watersons, etc. | New voices | TOPIC 12 T 125 |
| Ray Fisher, etc. | Bonny lass come o'er the burn | TOPIC 12 T 128 |
| Gordeanna McCulloch | New voices from Scotland | TOPIC 12 T 133 |
| | Folk song: an anthology | TOPIC TPS 145 |
| | A prospect of Scotland | TOPIC TPS 169 |
| | The Child ballads I and II | TOPIC 12 T 160/161 |
| Peggy Seeger and Ewan MacColl | The long harvest | DECCA DA 66–69 |
| Benjamin Britten | Serenade (Lyke wake dirge) | DECCA LXT 2941 |
| Ewan MacColl | English and Scottish popular ballads | FOLKWAYS FG 3509 |
| Lizzie Higgins | Princess of the thistle | TOPIC 12 T 185 |

# Scottish Literature: Bibliographical Notes

W. R. Aitken

The bibliography of Scottish literature is not particularly complex, but one has to know where to look for it. The problem to some extent arises from the difficulty of defining 'Scottish literature'. In many bibliographies and other reference works Scottish literature is treated as a part of English literature, and Scottish authors appear with English in such biographical dictionaries as *Everyman's Dictionary of literary biography: English and American* (3rd ed. Dent. 1969; Pan, 1972) and the excellent 'Authors Series' published by the H. W. Wilson Co. of New York: *British authors before 1800* (1952), *British authors of the 19th century* (1936), *Twentieth century authors* (1942; supplement 1955), and *World authors* (1975).

Scottish literature and Scottish authors are included in the following bibliographies:

> *The new Cambridge bibliography of English literature*, edited by George Watson and I. R. Willison. Vols. 1–4 (1969–74)—the 'most elaborate' of the general bibliographies, covering English literature from 600 to 1950.
> *Introductions to English literature*, edited by Bonamy Dobree. 5 vols. (rev. ed. 1966–9), particularly vol. 5, *The present age from 1920*, by David Daiches (1969).
> *The Pelican guide to English literature*, edited by Boris Ford. 7v. (1954–61; new impressions 1969–70).
> Bateson, F. W. *A guide to English literature* (2nd ed. 1967).
> Leclaire, Lucien. *A general analytical bibliography of the regional novelists of the British Isles, 1800–1950* (1954).

The last is supplemented for Glasgow by a comprehensive and skilfully annotated bibliography published by the Scottish Library Association:

> Burgess, Moira. *The Glasgow novel, 1870–1970* (1972).

There are useful sections on Scottish language and literature in two introductory Scottish bibliographies:

> *Scottish books: a brief bibliography for teachers and general readers* (Saltire Society, 1963)
> *Reader's guide to Scotland: a bibliography* (National Book League, 1968).

There are also excellent bibliographies in many histories of English and Scottish literature, among them:

Baugh, Albert C. *ed. A literary history of England* (2nd ed. 1967; also in 4v).
*The Oxford history of English literature.* 12v. (1945—in progress).
Wittig, Kurt. *The Scottish tradition in literature* (1958; repr. 1972).
Kinsley, James *ed. Scottish poetry: a critical survey* (1955).
Wood, H. Harvey. *Scottish literature* (1952)—a British Council pamphlet with bibliographical notes by Professor William Beattie, formerly librarian of the National library of Scotland.

For current bibliography there are again references for Scottish authors and for Scottish literature in general in the annual surveys of English literature:

*Annual bibliography of English language and literature.* 1920– .
*The year's work in English studies.* 1919– .

These have been supplemented since 1969 by three annual surveys of Scottish literature:

*Annual bibliography of Scottish literature*, published as a supplement to *The Bibliotheck*, a Scottish journal of bibliography and other topics, now edited from Stirling University Library.
*The year's work in Scottish literary studies*, published in *Scottish Literary News*, the newsletter of the Association for Scottish Literary Studies.
*Current Scottish prose and verse*, also in *Scottish Literary News*.

Reviews of new books of Scottish interest are to be found in *The Scotsman*, the *Glasgow Herald*, and the *Times Literary Supplement*, and in the Scottish literary magazines included elsewhere in this list. For reviews of books of particular relevance to schools *Teaching English*, the journal of teachers of English in Scotland, is indispensable.

For the reader who is looking for detailed bibliographical information on individual authors there are a number of separate author bibliographies. These can be identified from the *New Cambridge bibliography*, already mentioned, from A. J. Walford's *Guide to reference material* (2nd ed. vol. 3, 1970) and from T. H. Howard-Hill's *Bibliography of British literary bibliographies* (1969). The 'Writers and their Work' pamphlets, published by Longman for the British Council and National Book League, include brief bibliographies as well as introductory critical essays. (The pamphlets dealing with Scottish authors are included in this list.) For the bibliographies of more recent authors there is a useful guide, *A descriptive catalogue of the bibliographies of 20th century British writers* (1972), by Elgin W. Mellown, the bibliographer of Edwin Muir. A number of interesting checklists of modern Scottish writers have been published in *The Bibliotheck*, including Gibbon, Gunn, Linklater, MacDiarmid, Charles Murray and William Soutar.

Finally, notes—bibliographical, as well as biographical and critical—on many Scottish authors are to be found in the wide range of companions, dictionaries, guides and encyclopedias now available, among them:

*Cassell's Encyclopedia of world literature*, edited by J. Buchanan-Brown (2nd rev. ed. 3v. 1973).
*Contemporary poets of the English language*, edited by Rosalie Murphy (1970).
*Contemporary novelists*, edited by James Vinson (1972).
*Contemporary dramatists*, edited by James Vinson (1973).
*Guide to modern world literature*, by Martin Seymour-Smith (1973).
*Longman companion to English literature*, by Christopher Gillie (1972).
*Longman companion to twentieth century literature*, by A. C. Ward (1970).
*The Penguin companion to literature: Britain and the Commonwealth*, edited by David Daiches (1971).

*Twentieth century British literature: a reference guide and bibliography*, edited by Ruth Z. Temple and Martin Tucker (1968).
*Twentieth century writing: a reader's guide to contemporary literature*, edited by Kenneth Richardson (1969).
*Webster's New world companion to English and American literature*, edited by Arthur Pollard (1973).

# Appendix

# Appendix

A text-based programme of work on animals for early stage pupils.

## Fox and Wildcat

*Texts:*

Lea MacNally: *Highland Year*, Dent, 1968 (Pan, 1972)
Dent: pp. 16–20 (Pan: pp. 30–35) Foxes mating
Dent: pp. 20–22 (Pan: pp. 35–38) Habits of wildcat
Dent: pp. 57–62 (Pan: pp. 83–90) The fortunes of a fox family

Gavin Maxwell: *Ring of Bright Water*, Pan, 1972
pp. 25–27 Wildcats mating
pp. 28–29 Killing foxes

H. Mortimer Batten: *The Singing Forest*, Heinemann, 1955
pp. 80–83 Wildcat and deer

Joseph Jacobs (ed.): *Celtic Fairy Tales*, Bodley Head, 1970
pp. 230–235 'The Russet Dog'

Barbara Ker Wilson (ed.): *Scottish Folk Tales and Legends*, O.U.P., 1955
pp. 88–90 'The Fox and the Little Bannock'
pp. 91–92 'The Cock and the Fox'
pp. 93–94 'The Fox and the Bird'

Alexander Reid: 'The Kitten'
pp. 84–88 in *Scottish Short Stories*, Urquhart (ed.), Faber, 1957
or pp. 1–5 in *Ten Modern Scottish Stories*, Millar and Low (eds.), Heinemann, 1973

McPhedran and Kitchen (eds.): *Scottish Harvest*, Blackie, 1960
pp. 181–185 'Bright Eyes' (Foxes mating)
(from *String Lug the Fox*, David Stephen)

Buchan, N. (ed.): *101 Scottish Songs*, Collins, 1962
p. 137 'The Tod'

John Barbour: *The Bruce*, W. Skeat (ed.) O.U.P., 1968
Bk. XIX, lines 649–683, The Fox and the Salmon Fisher

Other Aids:
Films: *Three Fox Fables* (SCFL—D789)
      *Foxes* (SCFL—2DC 3359, No. 4 in Mammals of Scotland series)
      *British Carnivores* (SCFL—DC3258)

Record: *Cats and Dogs* (BBC Records, RED54M)

1. This set of material deals with the life of two Scottish predators and with human attitudes towards these animals. All of the items listed are currently in print, and are in some sense Scottish.

2. Probably with some selection the elements can be patterned satisfactorily in several different ways. Only trial will establish which items and which order work best. Some possible introductions to the study:

(a) Play without explanation a recording of the mating call of the vixen (*Cats and Dogs*).
*Assignment*: What on earth, can the noise be? Write down what you think of, what you feel, when you hear it.

(b) Start with a showing of the bizarre little film, *Three Fox Fables*, in which trained animals enact three of Aesop's tales (Black and white, 11 minutes).
*Assignment*: Write a short newspaper review of the film saying whether you like it or not, and why.

(c) Reid's 'The Kitten' could provide the starting point. Arguably this *must* come first because its fullest effect can only be experienced if the reader does not approach the story with the wildcat idea already in mind, but has it dawn on him gradually, through the storyteller's art.

Yet another possible introduction, with subsequent development is worked out below.

3. (a) Start from common language experience—the words *fox* and *cat* and their metaphoric extensions and collocations: foxy, wildcat strike, kittenish, bell-the-cat, vixen, catty, cub, cat-and-mouse etc.—dictionary work. Consider traditional names and Scottish names: Renard, Dan Russell, Gibb, Tod Lowrie, Baudrons.

(b) What do we imply when we call someone a Fox, a Vixen, a Cat, a Wildcat? What human personalities do we traditionally project on these animals? Why? Discussion here can lead to Aesop (*Aesop's Fables* translated by John Warrington, Dent's Children's Classics, 1961).
*Writing Assignment*: Compose your own cat or fox fable, with appropriate moral.

(c) A reading of Barbour's fable of the 'Fox and the Salmon Fisher'. Suggest an appropriate moral. A reading of some of the Scottish fox tales of Joseph Jacobs and Barbara Ker Wilson. What sort of personality has the fox in these?

*Possible Assignments*:
(i) These tales contain a good deal of dialogue and thus lend themselves to arrangement for taping and for dramatic interpretation. They are of Scottish provenance but the dialogue is notably un-Scots. A profitable approach might be to have pupils render them into a comfortable, informal, local idiom.
(ii) As simple narratives they might be presented, with captions, in a sequence of graphics for wall display. Both cat and fox are popular subjects with film and T.V. cartoonists. Discussion of popularity of animal cartoons.

(d) Learning and singing of the traditional Scots song, *The Tod*.

(e) Read Maxwell's account of fox killing and MacNally's narrative of the fortunes of a fox family.
Why do men kill foxes? Are you sorry for the foxes? What do you learn of fox

behaviour? What are the main similarities and differences in the two accounts? What can you tell about the two men from their stories?

(f) Make similar use of Stephen's and MacNally's descriptions of fox mating. Compare the fictional and non-fictional versions. Any similarities to *human* courtship?

*Writing Assignment:* Describe as accurately as you can any episode of animal behaviour (wild or tame) that you have seen.

(g) A showing and discussion of *Foxes* (Colour, 15 minutes).

(h) Read and discuss Reid's story 'The Kitten'. This story depends for its effect on a surprise ending, perhaps a rather contrived one. An interesting way of treating it therefore (particularly if there is only one copy) would be to read it to the class, stopping at the climactic sentences:

'Slowly, very slowly, the kitten backed towards him. The wind fought for it, delaying, almost holding the advance of the fire through the whins.'

Thereafter ask class to write their own endings to the story and discuss which is best.

However 'The Kitten' is presented, main points for discussion are:

the animal at bay (both mother and kitten),
maternal protectiveness,
drowning of kittens,
the clues to the kitten's origins,
the changing mood of the hired man,
the way in which the story ends.

(i) Read Maxwell's description of wildcat mating. In what ways is it relevant to Reid's story?

(j) What qualities of the wildcat emerge from MacNally's non-fictional and Mortimer Batten's fictional accounts? Which do you prefer? Why?

(k) Conclusion: A showing of *British Carnivores* (Colour, 10 minutes, includes fox and wildcat).

Final discussion and writing might involve some bringing together of the two creatures.

  (i) What have they in common? How do they differ?
 (ii) Some awareness of their points of contact and conflict with human beings.
(iii) Some discussion of how man *should* treat them. Protect them? Exterminate them? Control them? Ignore them?

4. This study could obviously be enriched and diversified by the use of 'non-Scottish' material, for example:

Kipling's 'Cat Who Walked by Himself'
The fox poems of Clare and Masefield.
The cat as a goading, demonic agent—'The Black Cat' (Poe), 'The Squaw' (Bram Stoker), 'A Case of Murder' (Scannell), 'The Captain's Cat' (Kirkconnell), 'The Cat Came Back' (Anon).

*The Fox Book* and *The Cat Book*, edited by Richard Shaw, Kay and Ward, 1972 and 1974, are delightfully illustrated simple anthologies of fox and cat lore for younger pupils.

*Town Fox, Country Fox*, Brian Vesey-Fitzgerald, Corgi, 1973 and *Wild Fox*, Roger Burrows, Pan, 1968, are useful sources of background information.

David Stephen: *Highland Animals*, H.I.D.B., 1974.

*Rufus the Story of a Fox* and *Scrap the Gentle Wild Cat*, Ernest Dudley, Muller, 1971 and 1974, are real-life accounts for younger pupils of 'tame' wild animals.

*Red Fox*, Charles G. D. Roberts, 1972, Longman Young Books: re-issue of classic story of the life cycle of a Canadian fox.

5. The teacher must judge from his knowledge of his pupils' abilities (and his own) whether it would be worthwhile attempting a simplified telling or reading of some Henryson, e.g. *The Fox, The Wolf and the Cadger*.

6. Out of print (at present) is another useful book on the topic:
*String Lug the Fox*, David Stephen (Collins).

### Extracts from *Highland Year* **L. MacNally,** *1972,* **Pan Books.**

1. *Pp. 30–35: Foxes mating*

In a winter largely spent out of doors one sees much of interest in glimpses of wild life denied to those who perforce spend most of their winter indoors.

A double line of tracks on the snow-sprinkled, partly frozen surface of a hill burn shows where a pair of otters have journeyed along together, diving into the ice-cold black waters where the burn was open. In deep snow one may see a furrow left by the short-legged otter as it journeyed for a time overland, literally ploughing its way along; an exhausting business it must be for an aquatic animal so absolutely out of its element.

One always remembers encounters with the elusive hill fox (and elusive the fox has to be in the Highlands with every hand against it), as on the day when, leading the pony at first light on a winter's morning, I came around a corner of the path to see a large yellow 'dog' approaching me, trotting sedately along the path in the still dim light. A yellow dog out here? Of course not! A large, yellowish dog fox! I dropped to the ground at once, as realization dawned, right under the pony's nose, trying to get my rifle from out of its cover. Hard to say who was the more surprised, the pony at my strange action, the fox at the sudden apparition of pony and stalker or myself at seeing the dog-like sedateness of the approaching fox. At all events, it was the fox that recovered first, to run unscathed up the hillside flanking the path, while I rose from my damp bed below the wondering pony's nose, a trifle chagrined but with one more memory to store.

Wild animals in fact use the hill paths surprisingly often, fox, wildcat, red deer and roe, otter occasionally, as their tracks in snow testify. On yet another winter morning it was a wildcat which met me almost face to face as I walked quietly along a narrow path.

The most amusing encounter I have had with a fox occurred while out hind-stalking, as a result of my startling a small herd of young stags. As they trotted in single file through the long heather of a sheltered hill face some way from me, the leader suddenly jumped almost straight up in the air, and out to one side, while from below his very hooves started out a very surprised fox, drowsily confused, almost rubbing its eyes one felt, rudely awakened from its snug heather bed. The fox ran behind a little ridge without noticing me, and judging that I had a chance to cut it off on the line it was taking I ran quickly forward. As I went, cautiously now, towards a commanding knoll ahead, so did an inquiring, sharp-snouted, long-whiskered visage, ears pricked, appear over its top, to give me one fleeting, quizzical look before vanishing, all sleepiness gone.

It is in January, and into February (their mating time), that foxes are at their most vocal, and this mainly in the long hours of winter darkness. From the rugged, tree-grown hill face across the river from my house I may then hear, at first light or in the gloaming, the unearthly love skirl of the vixen, or, more often, the *staccato* double bark of a questing dog fox. In the darkness of one January night I listened to a vixen skirling repeatedly, while from two different directions two suitors 'barked' in answer and drew nearer at each skirl. Dog foxes appear to outnumber vixens here, perhaps because the vixen is the more vulnerable at the annual den offensive at the cubbing time, and the hours of darkness probably cloak many a sharp-fanged struggle to decide who wins the 'red lady'. A shepherd here once told me of seeing a vixen coming through the hill escorted by a large dog fox, while close behind, too close for his own well-being, trailed a younger dog fox. Every so often the larger dog fox raced back and trounced the younger, but squeal and squirm though he did, the lure of the vixen was apparently too strong, for trail along he would, to be trounced soundly again whenever he ventured too close.

Vulpine courtship goes on all night long, the fox being largely nocturnal, and I have awakened with a start in the early hours of a January morning to hear all my terriers barking, with a 'let me get at you' note, while a vixen holds concert across the river.

The betraying snow at this time sometimes shows the neat double line of tracks of a mating pair as they 'honeymoon' through the hills, with here and there a flurry in the snow where they have presumably mated.

One of the questions which crop up every so often among people interested in wild life is whether dog fox ties to vixen, in mating, as with domesticated dog and bitch. I have never personally witnessed the mating of a pair of hill foxes, but a reliable colleague once told me of how he watched this occur, through his stalking glass against a background of snow, and that they definitely tied at the consummation of their mating. I have also been told of a shepherd who came suddenly into a little hollow, while out on the hill, to find himself almost on top of a pair of tied foxes, both of which he killed before they could separate. This, if true, must have been a million to one chance.

I do know as a definite fact of two stalkers, one of whom lay and watched through his stalking glass his colleague attempt to stalk, again in snow, a pair of tied foxes. As he watched, the foxes either heard or sensed the approaching enemy, separated at once and made themselves scarce. I would imagine that the sudden fright engendered in a Highland fox by the least suspicion of the proximity of their mortal enemy would be enough to cause the immediate separation and flight of even the most lovelorn pair.

Many people will no doubt experience a measure of revulsion in reading of how the emphasis seems to be on destroying the hill fox, even at its mating time. I would personally go on record as saying that while I regard the fox as possibly our most handsome and absolutely vital wild animal, its damage potential, particularly to the lambs of the hill sheep flocks, but also in a certain measure to the young of roe and red deer, must always lurk in the mind of shepherd and stalker. And the fox, with every hand against it, continues to thrive in the Highlands—a survival of the fittest indeed for the unwary or unfit seldom long survive the incessant persecution. Fox, eagle and deer: their lives and ways fascinate most of us, and stories are woven around them whenever stalkers forgather.

After their period of bliss the mated pair, I believe, roam around together inspecting possible den sites, until when, at last choosing one, they may or may not do some cleaning-out operations so as to have it in readiness for the vixen's cubbing later on in the year. It is apparent that more than one sand-hole is cleaned out at this time yet not used. The digging instinct is strongly instilled in foxes, and it may be that they cannot resist digging a bit at any sand-hole they pass, before rejecting it as unsuitable. Certainly in any one year we may find many sand-holes (fox-cleaned-out) for every one used.

Towards the end of January one year I lay watching a hind, her calf and her off-spring of the previous year, a young knobber with as yet only knobs covering the pedicles from which his antlers would later sprout, come slanting up the hill towards me, the hill streaked with the snow wreaths left by a recent thaw. When about fifty yards from me the hind suddenly shied off to one side and sniffed at the ground, then walked around in a wary, stiff-legged half-circle, outstretched nose near to the ground, and sniffed again. Whatever it was that had alarmed her was below my line of vision as I lay flat and watched, and, intrigued as I was, I could only conjecture. The hind then continued to come up towards me, crossing a snow wreath so hard-packed that she slipped once or twice, her hard hooves barely marking it. Up she came, passing me only five yards away, stopping occasionally to peer fixedly but without comprehension at my motionless and only half-hidden form. At one moment she looked long and questioningly, but my absolute immobility reassured her and she carried on beyond me for a step or two and began grazing. Her calf following twenty yards or so behind repeated the performance, as also did the knobber, redder in coat and more ragged-looking than the dark, sleek calf. Their suspicions were shorter lived than those of the hind, and they soon decided that the object, though strange, was harmless. All three fed in front of me for some time, the hind on a patch of heather, rapidly pulling at the tips, the others on grassy patches. So near was I that I could hear them pluck the herbage. Eventually they fed over the hill top above me and I then found that the cause of the hind's sudden shying aside was a dead vixen lying on a snow wreath. The ground was rock hard with frost that day and so I left the dead fox on top of a green knoll, intending to bury it when the ground was softer. I returned a few days later to find the fox vanished without trace, undoubtedly, I believe, 'lifted' by an eagle. Between fox and eagle there seems much animosity; I have had experience of more than one fox carcass eaten by eagles in the winter time, and have also seen fox feature as prey at eyries more than once. I know too, from a veteran keeper from an era where traps were often set for eagles, of how he went to visit a trap set in a known eyrie and found a fox caught in it. No doubt the fox had had his own reasons for visiting this eyrie. Certainly many eyries can be walked into, and I have little doubt that a bold, hungry fox might chance it if it thought it had the prospect of a helpless young eaglet in the parents' absence. There is also of course the scavenging aspect, the tempting smell of the prey which may be on the eyrie.

## 2. Pp. 35–38: Habits of wildcat

The wildcat has an unenviable reputation for utter ferocity, a reputation zealously fostered by the more sensational writers on wild life, to whom indeed sensationalism would seem to matter more than fact. The few brushes I have had with wildcats have not led me to worry overmuch about the possibility of being clawed to death by them; in fact, as with every wild animal on the British list, the wildcat will invariably take refuge in flight, *if it can*, rather than take aggressive action when confronted by a human. An animal absolutely cornered, again of practically any species (except perhaps the badger who often prefers to 'lie doggo') is a different matter. As a last resort here a rush may be made, apparently at its persecutors, a rush, however, which invariably will be made more with a desire to escape than anything else, but with potentially hurtful consequences should a collision occur.

I had a good illustration of this overwhelming desire to escape rather than be aggressive on the part of a wildcat when my terriers treed a large wildcat which had been raiding hen houses in my area one winter. The cat climbed right up among the thin, whippy branches at the top of a large birch tree, while my terriers yapped below, jumping and scrambling part way up the rough bole of the tree and sliding, rough claws scrabbling frantically, all the way down again. I had no gun or rifle with me and so there was nothing for it but to climb the tree. Walking-stick clutched firmly in one hand up I climbed, feeling, I can assure you, far less at home when I arrived among the whippy branches at the top than the cat could have done. As I arrived within reach of the cat, crouched facing me, I paused to take a better grip of my stick, and as I did so, so did the glaring cat spring, but not at my face as it could so easily have done. No, instead it sprang for the topmost branches of an adjacent birch tree, and missing them, fell to its death below.

In my area of Inverness-shire, where mountain hares have long been scarce, the wildcat relied, in pre-myxomatosis days, mainly on rabbit. At that time rabbit trapping and snaring was a winter occupation for professional trappers, and their bag here invariably contained around a dozen wildcats each winter, trapped or snared as they prowled about rabbit burrows or along rabbit runs. This habit of following rabbit runs led to the very unusual death of a wildcat here. Returning from the hill one winter evening I saw something dangling in the upper branches of a birch tree above my path. This tree was below a wide green flat which at that time held a sizeable warren and which in consequence was snared each winter. Going to investigate I found a large dead male wildcat dangling from a branch high up in the tree, a wire snare tight around its stomach. Caught around the waist by the snare, he had pulled out the snare peg in his struggle to get free, but in doing so had drawn the wire agonizingly tight around his middle. Running away from the pain and from the bouncing, terrifying snare peg inexorably bounding after him, he had at last rocketed up the tree, ever the ultimate feline refuge. There he had apparently jumped from branch to branch until he had succeeded in wrapping the wire around one, and in jumping for another one had been jerked up short and, so hanging, died.

I was lucky enough to watch a wildcat stalk a rabbit one winter afternoon, and was intrigued to see that it was stalking entirely by scent. Absolutely concentrated on the stalk, it did not see my arrival as I sank slowly into a crouch to watch developments. Just as it seemed that the elongated, flattened form of the cat would snap into its final electrifying spring, the rabbit flicked around and into the burrow at which it had been sitting. The frustrated cat arrived at the burrow almost at the rabbit's tail and thrust head and shoulders into it. I almost expected it to follow the rabbit down, but it probably knew from past experience just how fruitless this was likely to be. Emerging, it looked around and, spotting me now, made off. Possibly the rabbit had noticed some slight involuntary movement of mine which the cat, engrossed in the hunt, had not, and this had caused it to vanish down its burrow; or perhaps the tension of watcher and hunter had communicated itself to the intended victim. Whatever the cause, the cat was cheated of a meal, and I of seeing the successful conclusion of the wildcat's stalk.

Wildcats, unlike foxes, seldom eat carrion, even in the stress of winter's food scarcity. Their sharp but relatively small teeth are not adapted to tearing through deer hair or sheep's wool to get at the flesh below. I have, however, scared a wildcat from the carcass of a blackface ewe, and on investigation found that it had been skinning the head and eating the peelings of skin so obtained. Surely a very hungry cat to have reduced to such meagre pickings. Since then, however, I have found this very characteristic skinning of the head, no other part being touched, on sheep carrion. Had I not actually seen a wildcat at this I should still be puzzled as to what did it.

While the wildcat population throughout the Highlands is probably not high, it may well be higher than many people believe. Expert in utilizing cover, and, like the fox, highly nocturnal, they have ample cover in the rocks and trees of their favoured river glens, while on the bare, higher hills they have recourse to the drier hill drains or burn banks. Skulking along these often heather-overgrown pathways they will see, hear or scent humans while themselves remaining unseen. I was once able to show some friends a three-quarter grown wildcat curled up, snugly asleep, below the heather fringing the bank top of a small burn down which we were walking. A few yards on either side and we would have passed the sleeping cat with no awareness of its proximity. How often in fact must we pass wild life by, unaware of its nearness. Stoats are not particularly numerous around my home, more particularly since the myxomatosis-induced decline of the rabbit. They seem, however, to have the faculty of popping up at odd times and in odd places, such as the one my Labrador bitch chased far out on the hill, and which escaped by diving into the deep waters of a nearby burn and swimming across with all the aplomb of one born to this element. Or the one which I found dead, as prey, on the eyrie of a golden eagle. Or the one in full winter white which a friend of mine bolted from a hole in the mesh of his outdoor meat safe. That enterprising individual had had a good meal of venison as a reward for initiative.

### 3. Pp. 83–90: *The fortunes of a fox family*

A resourceful and beautiful predator, agile and quick-witted, the fox has fascinated its human pursuers for generations. In this I am no exception, and so when I had an opportunity in May a few years ago to piece together the fortunes of a fox family, partly from observation and partly from deduction and circumstantial evidence, I felt impelled to write of this. In order to preserve the continuity of the narrative I considered it better to put it down as if witnessed by some all-seeing, omniscient eye. This, however, is the only purely fanciful part; all the main facts are as noted in that year and are typical of what may happen in the annual fox-versus-humans warfare in the Highlands.

The grey light of the mild May dawning suited admirably the starkness of the dimly revealed Highland landscape. A bleak heather-clad ridge, its skyline indeterminate in the scuds of early morning mist which drifted along its top, dropped steeply in a grey rock-scattered slope to a burn brawling far below.

To the vixen, however, picking her way daintily among the rocks, a cock grouse in her jaws, the scene was homely enough, terrain to which she was well used. Her dog fox had gone missing shortly after they had mated earlier in that year, victim of man's unrelenting warfare on the Highland fox, and she had run alone thereafter until she had selected a den in which her cubs had been born in early April.

She had then had a very lean time, lacking a mate to forage and bring food to her while most of her attentions had to be fixed on her new-born, helpless cubs. A night or two after their birth she was reluctantly forced out by the need to forage for herself. Only half a mile or so from her den the rasping of wire upon wire caused her to halt and to make a cautious investigation. Caught in a sheep fence by the overlapping of the two top wires, which had ensnared one hind leg, she found a young stag almost *in extremis*, but with still enough strength to heave spasmodically at the ensnaring fence. Creeping closer, the vixen was seen by the trapped stag, who tossed his head wildly, causing the whole fence to jangle and vibrate in his renewed struggles.

The vixen decided discretion to be the better part of valour and blunted her hunger that night on a couple of fat voles and a very young rabbit caught venturing too far from its hill burrow. By the following night the stag was dead, and for many nights thereafter the vixen fed right royally on this food supply, so providentially near at hand, without which she might never have reared her cubs.

These cubs were now almost six weeks old and she was able to devote a major part of her time to hunting for them, a difficult enough task without a mate to share the burden. The cock grouse, held retriever-fashion in her jaws, was the result of a long night's foraging.

Almost at her den, a rocky cairn near the ridge top, the vixen suddenly bolted the last yard or so as a terrific spine-tingling swoosh seemed to split the air directly above her. Safely underground, she turned to snarl soundlessly at the golden eagle gaining height after its unsuccessful swoop. The eagle too had young to feed: only one, but one with a large appetite, and fox, to this particular eagle, was no novel prey.

Inside the den the vixen speedily forgot the eagle as five blue-grey furry bodies flung themselves forward to spit and quarrel over the grouse carcass. Leaving them to it she curled up in a corner, able to relax in underground security, and dozed, tired after weeks of single-handed ministering to her litter's needs. The cubs, their heads now beginning to assume the red fox colour in contrast to their still blue-grey body fur, continued to squabble until only a few feathers remained.

An hour or two later the eagle, now only a dot high above the ridge, saw the figure of the estate stalker toiling doll-like along the rock-strewn steepness of the glen-face, with two terriers running, minute-seeming, in front of him.

Lacking the eagle's all-embracing viewpoint, the first inkling the vixen had was the faint, far-off rasp of tackets on rock, an alien sound which galvanised her into instant alertness. Almost at once the hurtling entry of two eager, fox-hungry terriers caused the cubs to scatter in lightning reflex action into the cracks and slits which seamed the cairn's inside while the vixen bolted immediately. Activated by the over-riding instinct to save her own skin or by the desire to decoy the terriers after her, who knows? In this case it worked both ways.

The hard-running stalker, whose heedless terriers had far out-distanced him on first getting the irresistible scent of the den, was just in time to try a despairing and unavailing long shot as the vixen ran, terriers hard behind her. Cursing, slipping and slithering as he strove, dangerously, to hurry along the steep face, the stalker floundered after the rapidly disappearing terriers, themselves out-distanced by the fleet vixen, who, confused momentarily by the closeness of shot and pursuit, went to ground again in a long scattered cairn half a mile around the hill's shoulder. There she crouched for a moment, recovering her wits, and releasing, willy-nilly, the strong taint of fox alarm, until the scrabble of blunt claws and hard breathing at the cairn's entrance apprised her of the terrier's arrival.

Snaking noiselessly along in the darkness of the cairn's labyrinthine passage-ways, she left by a crack so tortuous and narrow that no terrier could follow. When the stalker arrived in a lather of sweat minutes later she was already well away, while the terriers were still underground, engrossed in the strong scent she had left behind. The stalker remained hopefully on guard above while his terriers took their time underground, alternatively coming to the surface and retiring underground again, striving to unravel the puzzle the vixen had left, eventually coming to the surface and making it plain they were no longer interested. Realizing the vixen had foiled his terriers and was no longer in the cairn, the stalker returned, cautiously, this time, to the first cairn, and the sudden re-entry of the terriers caught one cub which had prematurely ventured in to the main chamber. A nipped-off squeak told the man outside what had happened; but though he remained there for the rest of that cold, increasingly wet day his terriers had no further success, though they blunted claws and skinned muzzles in their efforts to penetrate into rocky cracks too narrow to admit of their entry. When he eventually left, the stalker, cold, tired and saturated, neglected, amazingly, to block the den's entrances, though he resolved to return next day with assistance to try again. He knew well enough that only an empty den would reward him, but hoped, optimistically, to pick up the trail of the decamped inmates and so find the fresh den.

From a commanding position in the long heather of the ridge top the vixen watched stalker and terriers go, and indeed stalked them for more than a mile on their homeward way before she satisfied herself that they were really departing. She then made her way back, fast, to her cubs, her long snout wrinkling in disgust at the doggy smell permeating her den. For a moment or so she sniffed gently at the dead cub and when she turned to leave the now dangerous den, followed by her four surviving cubs, she picked it up, as if unwilling to believe it dead, and carried it with her.

The small convoy journeyed far that night, through dripping heather, threading rock screes and somehow fording the burn in the glen's bottom *en route* to a new den. Small as they were the cubs were precociously agile, resting for brief intervals when their short legs tired. Well did the vixen know where she was leading them. Every likely cairn in the area had been prowled through at some time in her wanderings, and by the dreich wet dawning the tired cubs were again underground. But this time the family was split up, two cubs in a rocky slit of a cairn at the base of a low cliff, the other two in a scattered shallow cairn about four hundred yards farther on.

To this second cairn the vixen carried the dead cub, laying it down in an underground chamber. There it lay for a day or two until it became quite obvious to the mother that it would not stir again. She then carried it some fifty yards and buried it under a shallow covering of grey moss beneath an overhanging slab. Whether she consciously thought of it as a burial is doubtful. The instinct to dig, and to bury unwanted articles of prey, is very strong in the fox, and probably this alone motivated her action.

For three weeks the depleted family had peace. The stalker had indeed returned next day with a colleague and more terriers, but on a day of ceaseless rain and dangerously low mist, every burn swollen bank high, they had searched fruitlessly for hours before returning home drenched to the skin.

The cubs were much redder in coat now, growing apace and spending more time, when things were quiet, outside the dens, so that tracks began to be worn, visible to the observant eye. Occasionally they wandered far enough afield to visit each other, but in the main they kept to where the vixen had put them.

A strange clanking sound alerted the cubs of the shallower cairn one day causing them to scurry underground, the vixen being absent hunting. Peering out inquiringly they saw a lean dog fox dragging on one foreleg a small trap, its chain burnished bright by continual rubbing through heather and rock. Attracted by the increasingly odorous prey remains scattered around the den, he fed ravenously on some scraps of lamb and thereafter became an almost daily visitor, scavenging in his need for food. Since getting the trap on his foreleg earlier in the year he had existed precariously on carrion, deer and sheep carcasses mainly: but carrion was now scarce, the seasonal mortality peak being past for that year.

The den's immunity was soon to end. In her necessity to feed four perpetually ravenous cubs the vixen had killed lambs. These lambs had been missed eventually and the hue and cry was up. After a day or two's searching the two estate stalkers, with two terriers, came upon the rock-slit den on a day in early June. Here underground, in the deepness of its slit, were most of the noisome prey remains, and the terriers, perhaps confused by the nauseating stench inside, failed to locate the cubs, deep in the narrow fastness. Returning above ground, however, they almost at once picked up scent which a visiting cub from the other den had left only that morning.

The stalkers followed the eagerly questing terriers and were led straight to the farther shallower cairn where the more obvious prey remains lying above ground convinced them that this was the main den.

Excited barkings from underground, where the terriers had almost at once found a cub holed up in a narrow crack, further convinced them. Throughout the remainder of that day, however, stalemate prevailed, the dogs barking at the cubs but unable to get at or to bolt them, and the vixen obviously away from home. One stalker therefore remained at the den while his colleague returned the long miles home for warm clothing and provisions so as to remain at the den all night. Poking around among the rocks of the cairn, shaking his head bitterly every time he found the remains of lamb or grouse, the remaining stalker unearthed the body of the cub the vixen had buried and 'wondered exceedingly'.

Long after the first stalker had gone, the trap-encumbered dog fox came scavenging towards the den and, detecting the remaining stalker at once, retired, giving the den a wide berth. But fate was well and truly against him, for he ran straight into the returning stalker, who, rifle slung on back, laden with food and clothing, was nearing the den. The stalker, hearing the tell-tale rattle of the dragging chain, was alerted, so that fox and man saw each other almost simultaneously. As the fox turned to run so did food and clothing strew the heather, while the stalker frantically clawed for his slung rifle. Hampered as he was the dog fox was too slow in his retreat and a merciful bullet ended weeks of misery.

About 10 p.m. the vixen, quite unsuspicious, approached the den. She was within rifle shot of the one of the concealed stalkers, but to make quite sure he waited till she was closer. This decision undoubtedly saved the vixen, for as she momentarily vanished behind a hump of heather so did she get a taint of human on the fitful evening air, and at once taking cover in a convenient heather-concealed drain she did not reappear. She nevertheless stayed in the den's vicinity all night, and with the first glimmering of light worked closer and skirled once. As though waiting for this, both cubs shifted from inside the shallow cairn—an ill-fated move, for both were accounted for by the alerted watchers.

The vixen, as if realizing this, melted away before the strengthening daylight, accompanied by her two surviving cubs from the rock slit den. The stalkers left about 8 a.m., cold now, and tired, but reasonably certain that they had settled the issue. As indeed they had, as far as lamb-killing in that area went; for the vixen and her cubs, older now and capable of journeying farther, journeyed far out to the high ground before they stopped again, their home this time in the dry tunnels of a high peat hag. From now on their prey would be grouse and the occasional windfall of a new-born red deer calf, besides what other small prey in the shape of voles and fledgeling birds the high ground could muster. The vixen was luckier than many of her species in that she had herself survived and saved two cubs, while the stalkers were happy in having stopped the depredations on their ground; honours had been shared.

A day or two later the eagle, seeing the fox carcasses lying on the rocks of the cairn, carried them off one by one to its eyrie, where the hungry eaglet disdained them not. Little is wasted in the wilds at a time of year when many hungry youngsters are being reared by overworked parents.

126

## Extracts from *Ring of Bright Water* **Gavin Maxwell, Pan Books 1972.**

### 1. *Pp. 25–27: Wildcats mating*

English visitors who have come to Camusfeàrna are usually struck inarticulate by the desolate grandeur of the landscape and the splendour of pale blue and gold spring mornings, but they are entirely articulate in their amazement at the variety of wild life by which I am surrounded. Many Englishmen are, for example, quite unaware that wildcats are common animals in the West Highlands, and assume, when one refers to them, that one is speaking of domestic cats run wild, not of the tawny lynx-like ferals that had their den, that and every other year, within two hundred yards of my door. They bear as much relation to the domestic cat as does a wolf to a terrier; they were here before our first uncouth ancestors came to live in the caves below the cliffs, and they are reputedly untameable. When I first came here the estate on whose land the house stood had long waged war upon the wildcats, and a tree by the deer-larder of the lodge, four miles away, was decorated with their banded tails hanging like monstrous willow catkins from its boughs. Now, since the estate has turned from general agriculture to forestry, the wildcats are protected, for they are the worst enemy of the voles, who are in turn the greatest destroyers of the newly planted trees. Under this benign régime the number of wildcats has marvellously increased. The males sometimes mate with domestic females, but the offspring rarely survives, either because the sire returns to kill the kittens as soon as they are born, and so expunge the evidence of his peasant wenching, or because of the distrust in which so many humans hold the taint of the untameable. It is the wild strain that is dominant, in the lynx-like appearance, the extra claw, and the feral instinct; and the few half-breeds that escape destruction usually take to the hills and the den life of their male ancestors. An old river-watcher at Lochailort, who for some reason that now eludes me was known as Tipperary, told me that one night, awoken by the caterwauling outside, he had gone to the door with a torch and in its beam had seen his own black-and-white she-cat in the fierce embrace of a huge wild Tom. Thereafter he had waited eagerly for the birth of the kittens. When the time came she made her nest in the byre, and all that day he waited for the first birth, but at nightfall she had not yet brought forth. In the small hours of the morning he became conscious of piteous mewing at his door, and opened it to find his cat carrying in her mouth one wounded and dying kitten. In the dark background he heard a savage sound of worrying and snarling, and flashing his torch towards the byre he saw the wild tom in the act of killing a kitten. There was a green ember-glow of eyes, the flash of a big bottle-brush tail, and then the torch lit up nothing more but a pathetic trail of mangled new-born kittens. The single survivor, whom the mother had tried to carry to the house for sanctuary, died a few minutes later.

Wildcats grow to an enormous size, at least double that of the very largest domestic cat; this year there is one who leaves close to the house Homeric droppings of dimensions that would make an Alsation wolfhound appear almost constipated. It is comparatively rarely that one sees the animals themselves in the daytime, for they are creatures of the dark and the starlight. Once I caught one accidentally in a rabbit snare, a vast tom with ten rings to his tail, and that first year at Camusfeàrna I twice saw the kittens at play in the dawn, frolicking among the primroses and budding birch on the bank beyond the croft wall. They looked beautiful, very soft and fluffy, and almost gentle; there was no hint of the ferocity that takes a heavy annual toll of lambs and red-deer calves. Before man exterminated the rabbits they were the staple food both of the big leggy hill foxes and of these low-ground wildcats, and every morning I would see the heavily indented pad-marks in the sand at the burrow mouths. But now the rabbits have gone and the lambs are still here in their season, and where there has been a strong lamb at dusk, at dawn there are raw bones and a fleece like a bloodstained swab in a surgery. Then come the ravens from the sea cliffs, and the hooded crows, the ubiquitous grey-mantled scavengers, and by nightfall there is nothing to show for those slow months in the womb but white skeleton and a scrap of soft, soiled fleece that seems no bigger than a handkerchief.

### 2. Pp. 28–29: Killing foxes

It is the helpless red-deer calves that are the staple food of the hill foxes in June, and the young lambs in April and May, but what they live on for the rest of the year now that the rabbits have gone and the blue mountain hares become so scarce, remains a mystery to me. Possibly they eat more seldom than we imagine, and certainly mice form a large part of their diet. Some years ago I went out with a stalker to kill hill foxes after lambing time. The foxes' cairn was some two thousand feet up the hill, and we left at dawn, before the sun was up over hills that were still all snow at their summits, silhouetted against a sky that was apple-green with tenuous scarlet streamers. The cairn, a big tumble of granite boulders in a fissure of the hill-side, was just below the snowline, and by the time we reached it the sun had lifted in a golden glare over the high tops. The terriers went into the cairn and we shot the vixen as she bolted, and the dogs killed and brought out the five cubs; but of the dog fox there was no sign at all. We found his footprints in a peat hag a few hundred yards below, going downhill, and he had not been galloping but quietly trotting, so concluded that he had left the cairn some time before we had reached it and was probably unaware of anything amiss. We sat down under cover to wait for his return.

We waited all day. The spring breeze blew fresh in our faces from where the sea and the islands lay spread out far below us, and we could see the ringnet boats putting out for the first of the summer herring. All day there was very little movement on the hill; once a party of stags in early velvet crossed the lip of the corrie on our right, and once an eagle sailed by within a stone's throw, to bank sharply and veer off with a harsh rasp of air between the quills as his searching eye found us. In the evening it became chilly, and when the sun was dipping over the Outer Hebrides and the snow-shadows had turned to a deep blue, we began to think of moving. We were starting to gather up our things when my eye caught a movement in the peat hags below us. The dog fox was trotting up hill to the cairn, quite unsuspicious, and carrying something in his jaws. The rifle killed him stone dead at fifty yards, and we went down to see what he had been carrying; it was a nest of pink new-born mice—all he had found to bring home in a long day's hunting for his vixen and five cubs.

## Extract from *The Singing Forest* H. Mortimer Batten, Heinemann, 1955.

### Pp. 80–83: Wildcat and deer

Though there were always herds of deer scattered among the terraces on the green slopes of Corrie Rou, hinds with young calves rarely harboured there, for in addition to the nesting eagles, it was an impregnable stronghold of foxes and wildcats, occupying the cairns once held by bear and wolf. It is not wise to make one's home next to the dens of thieves, even though one may be well armed against them. So far as could be judged the valley of the hazels was reasonably free from such vermin, yet late one evening the agonised screaming of the roe-deer fawn brought the herd of red deer smartly to attention. The cry came from the rocky slope immediately above where they were resting, and instantly every hind set off in that direction, snorting defensively.

They had not gone far when a bundle of bristling and brindled fur came rolling down to meet them. It was a wildcat embracing the roe-deer fawn, her strong paws entwined about his neck and her terrible fangs at work behind his ears. As her terrified prey struck out she was cleverly using the impulses of his hindlegs to keep them rolling, for that was the easiest way to avoid the stabbing hoofs of the fawn's parents.

A small tiger she was, or something worse than a tiger for her size—forty-two inches from tip to tip. She was merely hanging on to the struggling fawn till such time as she could shift her grip to his throat, after which, having made sure of him, she would dart into the branches or the screes, glad enough to leave him to his parents till later, when she might return.

But the interception of the red deer upset her plans, for they were all round her in a moment. She shot off, and with a hissing snarl made for the nearest tree-trunk, which unfortunately for her was broken off seven feet from the ground. Still she reached the top, and crouched there, her broad ears laid back, her green eyes blazing furiously. Nowhere in the world could one have found a more complete picture of feline spite.

Corrie was with the herd, and in his eyes one might have seen the same dare-devil gleam as when he and Chang hunted the village cats together. At all events he knew, or thought he knew, a great deal about their gigantic gift for bluff, and he was not to be so easily bluffed. Frequently he had left Chang to do the baiting while he went quietly in from the other side, and this appeared a favourable opportunity for such tactics.

In their anger the hinds had no more sense than to gather round the head end of the cat, and she was cleverly holding them there by pouring the liquid fire of her tongue into their faces. Thus she would have held them until they were blind with fury, when she would have a chance to turn about and make for safer cover. But Corrie's chance came sooner. He slipped round to the other side of the stump, where the blunt black tip of her tail was curling ominously. There he made a terrific sky-hop, and his fore-hoofs struck the bristling body with a force that precipitated her head foremost straight into the faces of the assembled hinds.

Probably no one but Corrie knew how it happened, and the hinds did not all get off unscathed, for the cat broke her fall by clinging to the face of the one immediately below, and then she got her fangs and her terrible hind-legs to work. Another second and Starpoint's mother would have lost her eyes, but a second is a long time in such a rough-and-tumble, and Greyface did a thing one would hardly have expected of a stag. In an instant he had his teeth round the cat's neck, and had torn her loose. As she fell one of his hoofs went down in a deadly stab, completely disabling her.

The hinds finished it, all but the hind whose face was streaming blood. She had experienced enough and quietly crept away. But the others were thick on the spot, jostling each other for a place in the mêlée, and their hoofs thundered down in a veritable tattoo.

Nor was the roebuck absent. He had slipped in under them and was raining down blows with the rest; only his hindquarters visible in the general scrimmage. But Corrie recognised them, and he got in a double-fisted blow which knocked the roebuck clean out of the fight, without his even knowing who had hit him. Nor did they ever see him again, or his doe and her fawn, so they must have gone clear away from the valley of the hazels.

**Extract from** *Celtic Fairy Tales* **ed. Joseph Jacobs, Bodley Head, 1970.**

*Pp. 230–235:* '*The Russet Dog*'

Oh, he's a rare clever fellow, is the Russet Dog, the Fox, I suppose you call him. Have you ever heard the way he gets rid of his fleas? He hunts about and he hunts about till he finds a lock of wool: then he takes it in his mouth, and down he goes to the river and turns his tail to the stream, and goes in backwards. And as the water comes up to his haunches the little fleas come forward, and the more he dips into the river the more they come forward, till at last he has got nothing but his snout and the lock of wool. Down he dips his nose, and as soon as he feels his nose free of them, he lets go the lock of wool, and so he is free of his fleas. Ah, but that is nothing to the way in which he catches ducks for his dinner. He will gather some heather, and put his head in the midst of it, and then will slip downstream to the place where the ducks are swimming, for all the world like a piece of floating heather. Then he lets go, and— gobble, gobble, gobble, till not a duck is left alive. And he is as brave as he is clever. It is said that once he found the bagpipes lying all along, and being very hungry began to gnaw at them: but as soon as he made a hole in the bag, out came a squeal. Was the Russet Dog afraid? Never a bit: all he said was 'Here's music with my dinner.'

Now a Russet Dog had noticed for some days a family of wrens, off which he wished to dine. He might have been satisfied with one, but he was determined to have the lot—father and eighteen sons—but all so like that he could not tell one from the other, or the father from the children.

'It is no use to kill one son,' he said to himself, 'because the old cock will take warning and fly away with the seventeen. I wish I knew which is the old gentleman.'

He set his wits to work to find out, and one day seeing them all threshing in a barn, he sat down to watch them; still he could not be sure.

'Now I have it,' he said; 'well done the old man's stroke! He hits true,' he cried.

'Oh!' replied the one he suspected of being the head of the family, 'if you had seen my grandfather's strokes, you might have said that.'

The sly fox pounced on the cock, ate him up in a trice, and then soon caught and disposed of the eighteen sons, all flying in terror about the barn.

For a long time a Tod-hunter had been very anxious to catch our friend the fox, and had stopped all the earths in cold weather. One evening he fell asleep in his hut; and when he opened his eyes he saw the fox sitting very demurely at the side of the fire. It had entered by the hole under the door provided for the convenience of the dog, the cat, the pig, and the hen.

'Oh! ho!' said the Tod-hunter, 'now I have you.' And he went and sat down at the hole to prevent Reynard's escape.

'Oh! ho!' said the fox, 'I will soon make that stupid fellow get up.' So he found the man's shoes, and putting them into the fire, wondered if that would make the enemy move.

'I shan't get up for that, my fine gentleman,' cried the Tod-hunter.

Stockings followed the shoes, coat and trousers shared the same fate, but still the man sat over the hole. At last the fox having set the bed and bedding on fire, put a light to the straw on which his jailer lay, and it blazed up to the ceiling.

'No! that I cannot stand,' shouted the man, jumping up; and the fox, taking advantage of the smoke and confusion, made good his exit.

But Master Rory did not always have it his own way. One day he met a cock, and they began talking.

'How many tricks canst thou do?' said the fox.

'Well,' said the cock, 'I could do three; how many canst thou do thyself?'

'I could do three score and thirteen,' said the fox.

'What tricks canst thou do?' said the cock.

'Well,' said the fox, 'my grandfather used to shut one eye and give a great shout.'

'I could do that myself,' said the cock.

'Do it,' said the fox. And the cock shut one eye and crowed as loud as ever he could, but he shut the eye that was next the fox, and the fox gripped him by the neck and ran away with him. But the wife to whom the cock belonged saw him and cried out, 'Let go the cock; he's mine.'

'Say, "Oh sweet-tongued singer, it is my own cock", wilt thou not?' said the cock to the fox.

Then the fox opened his mouth to say as the cock did, and he dropped the cock, and he sprung up on the top of a house, and shut one eye and gave a loud crow.

But it was through that very fox that Master Wolf lost his tail. Have you never heard about that?

One day the wolf and the fox were out together, and they stole a dish of crowdie. Now in those days the wolf was the biggest beast of the two, and he had a long tail like a greyhound and great teeth.

The fox was afraid of him, and did not dare to say a word when the wolf ate the most of the crowdie, and left only a little at the bottom of the dish for him, but he determined to punish him for it; so the next night when they were out together the fox pointed to the image of the moon in a pool left in the ice, and said:

'I smell a very nice cheese, and there it is, too.'

'And how will you get it?' said the wolf.

'Well, stop you here till I see if the farmer is asleep, and if you keep your tail on it, nobody will see you or know that it is there. Keep it steady. I may be some time coming back.'

So the wolf lay down and laid his tail on the moonshine in the ice, and kept it for an hour till it was fast. Then the fox, who had been watching, ran in to the farmer and said: 'The wolf is there; he will eat up the children—the wolf! the wolf!'

Then the farmer and his wife came out with sticks to kill the wolf, but the wolf ran off leaving his tail behind him, and that's why the wolf is stumpy-tailed to this day, though the fox has a long brush.

One day shortly after this Master Rory chanced to see a fine cock and fat hen, off which he wished to dine, but at his approach they both jumped up into a tree. He did not lose heart, but soon began to make talk with them, inviting them at last to go a little way with him.

There was no danger, he said, nor fear of his hurting them, for there was peace between men and beasts, and among all animals.

At last after much parleying the cock said to the hen, 'My dear, do you not see a couple of hounds coming across the field?'

'Yes,' said the hen, 'and they will soon be here.'

'If that is the case, it is time I should be off,' said the sly fox, 'for I am afraid these stupid hounds may not have heard of the peace.'

And with that he took to his heels and never drew breath till he reached his den.

Now Master Rory had not finished with his friend the wolf. So he went round to see him when his stump got better.

'It is lucky you are,' he said to the wolf. 'How much better you will be able to run now you haven't got all that to carry behind you.'

'Away from me, traitor!' said the wolf.

But Master Rory said: 'Is it a traitor I am, when all I have come to see you for is to tell you about a keg of butter I have found?'

After much grumbling the wolf agreed to go with Master Rory.

So the Russet Dog and the wild dog, the fox and the wolf, were going together; and they went round about the sea-shore, and they found the keg of butter, and they buried it.

On the morrow the fox went out, and when he returned in he said that a man had come to ask him to a baptism. He arrayed himself in excellent attire, and he went away, and where should he go but to the butter keg; and when he came home the wolf asked him what the child's name was; and he said it was HEAD OFF.

On the morrow he said that a man had sent to ask him to a baptism, and he reached the keg and he took out about half. The wolf asked when he came home what the child's name was.

'Well,' said he, 'it is a queer name that I myself would not give to my child, if I had him; it is HALF AND HALF.'

On the morrow he said that there was a man there came to ask him to a baptism again; off he went and he reached the keg, and he ate it all up. When he came home the wolf asked him what the child's name was, and he said it was ALL GONE.

On the morrow he said to the wolf that they ought to bring the keg home. They went, and when they reached the keg there was not a shadow of the butter in it.

'Well, thou wert surely coming here to watch this, though I was not,' quoth the fox.

The other one swore that he had not come near it.

'Thou needst not be swearing that thou didst not come here; I know that thou didst come, and that it was thou that took it out; but I will know it from thee when thou goest home, if it was thou that ate the butter,' said the fox.

Off they went, and when they got home he hung the wolf by his hind legs, with his head dangling below him, and he had a dab of the butter and he put it under the wolf's mouth, as if it was out of the wolf's belly that it came.

'Thou red thief!' said he, 'I said before that it was thou that ate the butter.'

They slept that night, and on the morrow when they rose the fox said:

'Well, then, it is silly for ourselves to be starving to death in this way merely for laziness; we will go to a town-land, and we will take a piece of land in it.'

They reached the town-land, and the man to whom it belonged gave them a piece of land the worth of seven Saxon pounds.

It was oats that they set that year, and they reaped it and they began to divide it.

'Well, then,' said the fox, 'wouldst thou rather have the root or the tip? Thou shalt have thy choice.'

'I'd rather the root,' said the wolf.

Then the fox had fine oaten bread all the year, and the other one had fodder.

On the next year they set a crop; and it was potatoes that they set, and they grew well.

'Which wouldst thou like best, the root or the crop this year?' said the fox.

'Indeed, thou shalt not take the twist out of me any more; I will have the top this year,' quoth the wolf.

'Good enough, my hero,' said the fox.

Thus the wolf had the potato tops, and the fox the potatoes. But the wolf used to keep stealing the potatoes from the fox.

'Thou hadst best go yonder, and read the name that I have in the hoofs of the grey mare,' quoth the fox.

Away went the wolf, and he begun to read the name; and on a time of these times the white mare drew up her leg, and she broke the wolf's head.

'Oh!' said the fox, 'it is long since I heard my name. Better to catch geese than to read books.'

He went home, and the wolf was not troubling him any more.

But the Russet Dog found his match at last, as I shall tell you.

One day the fox was once going over a loch, and there met him a little bonnach, and the fox asked him where he was going. The little bonnach told him he was going to such a place.

'And whence camest thou?' said the fox.

'I came from Geeogan, and I came from Cooaigean, and I came from slab of the bonnach stone, and I came from the eye of the quern, and I will come from thee if I may,' quoth the little bonnach.

'Well, I myself will take thee over on my back,' said the fox.

'Thou'lt eat me, thou'lt eat me,' quoth the little bonnach.

'Come then on the tip of my tail,' said the fox.

'Oh no! I will not; thou wilt eat me,' said the little bonnach.

'Come into my ear,' said the fox.

'I will not go; thou wilt eat me,' said the little bonnach.

'Come into my mouth,' said the fox.

'Thou wilt eat me that way at all events,' said the little bonnach.

'Oh no, I will not eat thee,' said the fox. 'When I am swimming I cannot eat anything at all.'

He went into the fox's mouth.

'Oh! ho!' said the fox, 'I may do my own pleasure on thee now. It was long ago said that a hard morsel is no good in the mouth.'

The fox ate the little bonnach. Then he went to a loch, and he caught hold of a duck that was in it, and he ate that.

He went up to a hillside, and he began to stroke his sides on the hill.

'Oh, king! how finely a bullet would spank upon my rib just now.'

Who was listening but a hunter.

'I'll try that upon thee directly,' said the hunter.

'Bad luck to this place,' quoth the fox, 'in which a creature dares not say a word in fun that is not taken in earnest.'

The hunter put a bullet in his gun, and he fired at him and killed him, and that was the end of the Russet Dog.

**Extracts from** *Scottish Folk-Tales and Legends* **retold by Barbara Ker Wilson Oxford University Press, 1954.**

1. *Pp. 88–90: 'The Fox and the Little Bannock'*

There was once a good housewife who lived in a little white cottage at the top of a steep hill. One day she made three bannocks for her husband's supper: a big bannock, a middle-sized bannock, and a little bannock; and when she had taken them out of the oven, she put them on a platter to cool. The big bannock and the middle-sized bannock were quite content to remain where they were; but the little bannock, who was baked brown and crusty and smelt very good to eat, thought to himself:

'Why should I remain here and be eaten by the good man for his supper? I will go out into the world and seek a better fortune.'

So he humped right off the platter and rolled to the cottage door. Now, as I have said, the cottage stood at the top of a steep hill; and before he could stop to think, the little bannock found himself rolling-rolling-rolling all the way down it.

'That was a quick escape, and no mistake!' he puffed. And then he gasped in dismay. For a river ran by the foot of the hill, and there was no way to get across it.

Just then who should come into sight but the red-brown fox, with his sharp white teeth and crafty eyes.

'Good day, little bannock,' said the Fox. 'Can it be that you are wanting to cross to the other side of the river?'

'Good day, Fox,' replied the little bannock a wee bit nervously, for the Fox had such *very* sharp white teeth, and his eyes were *so* crafty. 'Indeed, I am wanting to cross to the other side of the river.'

'I will take you over,' said the Fox.

'Och, no!' said the little bannock. 'If I were to let you do that, you would eat me for sure.'

'Eat you!' replied the Fox, pretending to be hurt at such a suggestion. 'Of course I won't eat you. Come on to the tip of my tail, and I will swim across the water.'

Well now, the little bannock thought that he surely ought to be safe enough if he was carried over like that; so he jumped on to the very tip of the Fox's bushy red brush, and they plunged into the river together.

When they were about a quarter of the way across, the water got deeper, and the Fox said:

'Come on to my back, little bannock, for you are getting wet.'

And the little bannock hopped onto the Fox's back.

When they were half-way across, the water grew deeper yet, and the Fox said:

'Come and perch between my ears, little bannock, for you are getting wet.'

And the little bannock hopped up between the Fox's ears.

When they were three-quarters of the way across, the water was the deepest it had ever been, and the Fox said:

'Come on to my nose, little bannock, for you are getting wet.'

And the little bannock hopped on to the tip of the Fox's long, pointed nose. Oh, foolish little bannock! For the Fox immediately threw back his head and snapped him all up. And by the time the farther side of the river was reached, there was only the crafty old Fox licking his lips with his long pink tongue, and no sign at all of the crusty little brown bannock who had tasted so very good to eat!

## 2. Pp. 91–92: 'The Cock and the Fox'

One day the red-brown fox with his crafty eyes and bushy tail came slinking over the hill-side and stole away a fine, plump Cock from the farmer's yard.

At once there was a terrible commotion, and all the people came running out to chase the Fox, who set off for his lair as fast as he could go, with the Cock held firmly in his mouth.

Now Cockie-leerie-law was quite determined that he would not become the Fox's dinner, and he tried to think of a way to get the thief to open his mouth and let him fall. So he spoke up in a flattering tone and said:

'Are they not foolish, Fox, to be chasing the likes of you! For they can never hope to catch up with you.'

The Fox was pleased at these words, for he was vain as well as crafty; and Cockie-leerie-law continued:

'All the same, although they cannot hope to catch you, it is not the thing at all to have a whole lot of people running along behind and crying "Stop, thief!" Why do you not call out to them: "It is my own cock that is here, and not one that I have stolen at all!" Then they will all turn back and you will be able to go on your way to peace.'

The Fox thought this was a very good idea, and without more ado he opened his mouth, threw up his head and sang out:

'She-mo-haolach-ha-n-a-han!'

And while he did so, Cockie-leerie-law seized his opportunity and, with his bright-red comb flopping over one bright eye, ran straight back to the farm-yard.

## 3. Pp. 93–94: 'The Fox and the Bird'

A kestrel hawk was dozing on the sun-warmed stones of a river-bank when the cunning red-brown Fox slunk upon him unawares, and with one pounce caught and held him in cruel jaws.

'Oh! Don't devour me,' cried the Hawk; 'if you will only let me go, I will lay for you an egg as big as your head!'

At this the Fox thought he had indeed got hold of a bird of birds; and, eager to have such a marvellous treasure for himself, he immediately loosened his grasp of the bird's soft throat.

Forthwith the kestrel flew up into the safety of a leafy tree-branch, where safe from further injury, he began to mock the foolish Fox.

'I will not lay for you an egg as big as your head,' said the bird, 'for I cannot do it. But I will give you three pieces of advice, and if you will observe them, they will do you more good in the future.

'First: never believe an unlikely story from an unreliable authority. Second: never make a great fuss about a small matter. And third'—the bird looked down at the hungry Fox and paused—'third: whatever you get a hold of, take a firm grip of it.'

And saying this, he flew away and left the Fox with empty jaws.

**Extract from** *Ten Modern Scottish Stories* **ed. Robert Millar and J. T. Low Heinemann.**

ALEXANDER REID

*The Kitten*

The feet were tramping directly towards her. In the hot darkness under the tarpaulin the cat cuffed a kitten to silence and listened intently.

She could hear the scruffling and scratching of hens about the straw-littered yard; the muffled grumbling of the turning churn in the dairy; the faint clink and jangle of harness from the stable—drowsy, comfortable, reassuring noises through which the clang of the iron-shod boots on the cobbles broke ominously.

The boots ground to a halt, and three holes in the cover, brilliant, diamond-points of light, went suddenly black. Couching, the cat waited, then sneezed and drew back as the tarpaulin was thrown up and glaring white sunlight struck at her eyes.

She stood over her kittens, the fur of her back bristling and the pupils of her eyes narrowed to pin-points. A kitten mewed plaintively.

For a moment, the hired man stared stupidly at his discovery, then turned towards the stable and called harshly: 'Hi, Maister! Here a wee.'

A second pair of boots clattered across the yard, and the face of the farmer, elderly, dark and taciturn, turned down on the cats.

'So that's whaur she's been,' commented the newcomer slowly.

He bent down to count the kittens and the cat struck at him, scoring a red furrow across the back of his wrist. He caught her by the neck and flung her roughly aside. Mewing she came back and began to lick her kittens. The Master turned away.

'Get rid of them,' he ordered. 'There's ower mony cats aboot this place.'

'Aye, Maister,' said the hired man.

Catching the mother he carried her, struggling and swearing, to the stable, flung her in, and latched the door. From the loft he secured an old potato sack and with this in his hand returned to the kittens.

There were five, and he noticed their tigerish markings without comprehending as, one by one, he caught them and thrust them into the bag. They were old enough to struggle, spitting, clawing and biting at his fingers.

Throwing the bag over his shoulder he stumped down the hill to the burn, stopping twice on the way to wipe the sweat that rickled down his face and neck, rising in beads between the roots of his lint-white hair.

Behind him, the buildings of the farm-steading shimmered in the heat. The few trees on the slope raised dry, brittle branches towards a sky bleached almost white. The smell of the farm, mingled with peat-reek, dung, cattle, milk, and the dark tang of the soil, was strong in his nostrils, and when he halted there was no sound but his own breathing and the liquid burbling of the burn.

Throwing the sack on the bank, he stepped into the stream. The water was low, and grasping a great boulder in the bed of the burn he strained to lift it, intending to make a pool.

He felt no reluctance at performing the execution. He had no feelings about the matter. He had drowned kittens before. He would drown them again.

Panting with his exertion, the hired man cupped water between his hands and dashed it over his face and neck in a glistening shower. Then he turned to the sack and its prisoners.

He was in time to catch the second kitten as it struggled out of the bag. Thrusting it back and twisting the mouth of the sack close, he went after the other. Hurrying on the sun-browned grass, treacherous as ice, he slipped and fell headlong, but grasped the runaway in his outflung hand.

It writhed round immediately and sank needle-sharp teeth into his thumb so that he grunted with pain and shook it from him. Unhurt, it fell by a clump of whins and took cover beneath them.

The hired man, his stolidity shaken by frustration tried to follow. The whins were thick and, scratched for his pains, he drew back, swearing flatly, without colour or passion.

Stooping he could see the eyes of the kitten staring at him from the shadows under the whins. Its back was arched, its fur erect, its mouth open, and its thin lips drawn back over its tiny white teeth.

The hired man saw, again without understanding, the beginnings of tufts on the flattened ears. In his dull mind he felt a dark resentment at this creature which defied him. Rising, he passed his hand up his face in heavy thought, then slithering down to the stream, he began to gather stones. With an armful of small water-washed pebbles he returned to the whins.

First he strove to strike at the kitten from above. The roof of the whins was matted and resilient. The stones could not penetrate it. He flung straight then—to maim or kill—but the angle was difficult and only one missile reached its mark, rebounding from the ground and striking the kitten a glancing blow on the shoulder.

Kneeling, his last stone gone, the hired man watched, the red in his face deepening and thin threads of crimson rising in the whites of his eyes as the blood mounted to his head. A red glow of anger was spreading through his brain. His mouth worked and twisted to an ugly rent.

'Wait—wait', he cried hoarsely, and, turning, ran heavily up the slope to the trees. He swung his whole weight on a low-hanging branch, snapping it off with a crack like a gun-shot.

Seated on the warm, short turf, the hired man prepared his weapon, paring at the end of the branch till the point was sharp as a dagger. When it was ready he knelt on his left knee and swung the branch to find the balance. The kitten was almost caught.

The savage lance-thrust would have skewered its body as a trout is spiked on the beak of a heron, but the point, slung too low, caught in a fibrous root and snapped off short. Impotently the man jabbed with his broken weapon while the kitten retreated disdainfully to the opposite fringe of the whins.

In the slow-moving mind of the hired man the need to destroy the kitten had become an obsession. Intent on this victim, he forgot the others abandoned by the burn side; forgot the passage of time, and the hard labour of the day behind him. The kitten, in his distorted mind, had grown to a monstrous thing, centring all the frustrations of a brutish existence. He craved to kill . . . .

But so far the honours lay with the antagonist.

In a sudden flash of fury the man made a second bodily assault on the whins and a second time retired defeated.

He sat down on the grass to consider the next move as the first breath of the breeze wandered up the hill. As though that were the signal, in the last moments of the sun, a lark rose, close at hand, and mounted the sky on the flood of its own melody.

The man drank in the coolness thankfully, and, taking a pipe from his pocket, lit the embers of tobacco in the bowl. He flung the match from him, still alight, and a dragon's tongue of amber flame ran over the dry grass before the breeze, reached a bare patch of sand and flickered out. Watching it, the hired man knitted his brows and remembered the heather-burning, and mountain hares that ran before the scarlet terror. And he looked at the whins.

The first match blew out in the freshening wind, but at the second the bush burst into crackling flame.

The whins were alight on the leeward side and burned slowly against the wind. Smoke rose thickly, and parks and lighted shivers of wood sailed off on the wind to light new fires on the grass of the hillside.

Coughing as the pungent smoke entered his lungs, the man circled the clump till the fire was between him and the farm. He could see the kitten giving ground slowly before the flame. He thought for a moment of lighting this side of the clump also and trapping it between two fires; took his matches from his pocket, hesitated, and replaced them. He could wait.

Slowly, very slowly, the kitten backed towards him. The wind fought for it, delaying, almost holding the advance of the fire through the whins.

Showers of sparks leaped up from the bushes that crackled and spluttered as they burned, but louder than the crackling of the whins, from the farm on the slope of the hill, came another noise—the clamour of voices. The hired man walked clear of the smoke that obscured his view and stared up the hill.

The thatch of the farmhouse, dry as tinder, was aflare.

Gaping, he saw the flames spread to the roof of the byre, to the stables; saw the farmer running the horses to safety, and heard the thunder of hooves as the scared cattle, turned loose, rushed from the yard. He saw a roof collapse in an uprush of smoke and sparks, while a kitten, whose sire was a wild cat, passed out of the whins unnoticed and took refuge in a deserted burrow.

From there, with cold, defiant eyes, it regarded the hired man steadfastly.


**Extract from** *Scottish Harvest* **ed. McPhedran and Kitchen, 1960, Blackie.**

DAVID STEPHEN

*Bright Eyes*

Across the wind-ruffled surface of the loch a silver pathway led away to the moon, and the shining water was pencilled with shadows which were ripples curling inshore. Through the sere, whispering threshes in the shallows thin ice crept out to meet the lap of water. The pines crowding down to the east shore were hard and black against the moon. Ducks dozed unseen in the ripple shadows—mallard and goldeneye, teal, tufted and shoveler; and grey geese slept a waking sleep, fearing the otter they had seen on the shore at the going down of the sun. A barn owl flying over the loch twelve feet over his shadow saw the otter dive where the pines made the water dark, and skirled his wild lament as he wafted overhead on wings as noiseless as sleep.

The otter swam inshore under his own moon-sparkling bubble chain, to hide in the reeds till lifted heads went down again. He was hungry after a day's fasting. There were no fish in the loch and he could not hope to reach the river till the following day. So he was prepared to try his luck at sleeping duck. Near the bank he paused, listening, with chin on rump and rudder coiled round his breast. His lack-lustre, water-dimmed eyes glared savagely and his fur was oil-sleek in the moonshine. He left the water as the barn owl flapped along the shore. On the point of snarling at the ghostly bird, he spun round with a grimace and a twitch of whiskers when his nose found the taint of fox. Out of the shadow of a blaeberry-cushioned hillock, faced with white, lichened rock, came a big fox with a gigantic brush and teeth flashing pearl-white in the moonlight.

With the wind in his favour, the fox had early warning of the otter's presence, while his own was unsuspected. And he came prepared to chop. But when he saw the size of the otter he slowed at once to a dignified walk and veered away, trying to look unconcerned. The otter sat for a fraction of a second with one forepaw uplifted, and his lips drawn so far back from his teeth that the skin folds almost hid his eyes. Then he twisted away into the reeds, his entry betrayed by the twinkle of the shattering ice-film. For some moments he crouched among the broken reeds, with only his eyes and nostrils above the water, while the fox stood rigid. When the fox moved away he swam into deeper water and disappeared.

String Lug walked leisurely towards the dark pine strip, his pads making scarcely a whisper on the frosted grass.

A tawny owl hooted as he entered the strip. She left her perch, wicking wheezily when she saw the fox, and crossed the moon's face when she topped the trees. String Lug saw her silhouetted against the moon, big-headed and front-heavy, mewing like a cat till she pitched in another tree farther down the woodside. He stood like an image while she hooted from her new perch—a long drawn-out, catenated, bubbling cry, which was the very voice of the solitude. How well he knew that cry! He had heard it almost nightly throughout his life, but on that night it made him feel at home.

In the moon-misted gloom, gold and green lights, which were the eyes of sheep, flashed on and off, and he heard the thud of hooves in flight. Pigeons, crows, and pheasants shuffled on perches above his head, but no bird took the air at his passing.

On the east side of the wood was a thick hedge, hiding the fence which topped the bank. From the deepest part of the hedge, where briars sent tendrils over the top, twin crimson stars flickered suddenly. The stars kept even eye-distance apart and held steady at fox height. The lights flashed off when String Lug minced forward, and he heard the rustle of a leaf touched by a hasty foot. The smell of the dog fox sent an electric shock through him. Rushing to the spot, he burst into the thorn tangle and sniffed at the soiling. When he pushed through into the open he was set for war.

Ere his brush was quite clear of the dragging thorns he stopped short, with head down and lips lifted. With eyes flaming green in the full glare of the moon, he pondered the strange spectacle before him. Fifty yards away, in a mossy depression between high peat banks, three dog foxes were walking in circles, with brushes rigid, rumps arched and heads askew. The birses of all three were up and String Lug could see, every now and again, the fleeting flash of ivory. It was the first time he had seen such a party; but he knew it was a mating brawl and that somewhere not very far away would be the vixen over which they were arguing.

In his own veins the fire kindled quickly to fighting heat. Eager to miss nothing of the spectacle, he leaned forward into the wind like a dog feeling for the scent of a hidden bird. Suddenly he relaxed and sat down on his hunkers, to reflect on his mode of entry into the drama. He had the advantage of being on the wrong side of the wind for the others to smell him, so he had some little time in which to make up his mind.

As if at a prearranged signal the foxes stopped circling and rushed at each other in a mad scramble. String Lug heard a double yap, the quick intake of breath and the sudden gasp of air expelled by the shock of bodies. Brushes swiped wildly at eyes. Teeth flashed and clicked and foxes spat hair, while their musk scent came stronger to String Lug's nostrils. The smallest beast fell while the other two reared and met forepaws to forepaws and teeth to teeth. They made much show of worrying without unduly disturbing each other's whiskers, for they were not yet in really savage mood and had little stomach for a serious grapple. But they were warming up to it. String Lug knew they were fanning hate and courage and that soon their cut-and-run thrusts, their heel-nipping and eye-wiping, would give way to more serious fighting, unless two of them quit before then. He decided the moment had come to intervene.

He crawled to the edge of the peat bank without being seen, and grinned. He could smell the vixen beyond the opposite bank. The wind combed the fur of his ruff, shedding it like corn falling before a reaper. He rose when the foxes joined in another general mix-up. Pointing his nose to the sky he barked—three harsh yaps which ripped the air and froze the brawling foxes in their tracks. Their breath hung in puffs of white vapour above their heads, and their hanging tongues drooled warm sweat. The vixen squalled and String Lug leaped, and the moon smiled sardonically down.

The encounter was brief, the action swift, and String Lug was touching noses with the vixen before the dog foxes had time to pull in their tongues. He laid open the mask of one with a lightning slash of teeth, shouldered the smallest beast, which was a mangy cur with bare, dry patches on thighs and flanks, and walloped the third hard across the face with his gritty brush. Before they could unite against him, he was up the opposite bank and whimpering to the vixen where she sat in deep heather, chewing the fleshy thigh bone of a water-hen. She clicked her incisor teeth at him, parted her lips and snarled at him through locked molars. String Lug cringed, turning his face side on to her, expecting a nip in the cheek or a puncture in his upright ear. Instead, he heard the clash of teeth at his big tendon, and wheeled to meet the assault. It was the fox whose eyes he had wiped a few moments before.

String Lug's turn and counter-attack were carried through in one perfectly timed movement and his teeth scored a red furrow on the other's cheek. The beast danced back with a startled yelp, twisted away, and fled with rump down and brush curled under his belly. The others, coming in on a converging run to the assault, drew back when he reached at them with teeth bared and brush gathered for hitting. They bolted ignominiously in opposite directions, making as much noise as a duck pattering on mud. When String Lug turned back the vixen was already loping across the heather, a grey, gliding shape in the unclouded moonshine.

Throughout the night String Lug pursued and wooed her, skirmishing incessantly with two foxes which had still some courage left for arguing. One of them was the mangy dog who, like so many with similar afflictions, was a most persistent suitor. String Lug left him with several additional bare patches not caused by mange. By daylight he had won the battle and the lady. His bad temper vanished and the ache in his heart was stilled. And when the sun rose at last, sending waves of palest pink, washing over the barred lilac and saffron of the morning sky, he lay down beside her in a grouse butt and licked her willing ears.

from *String Lug the Fox*

## The Tod

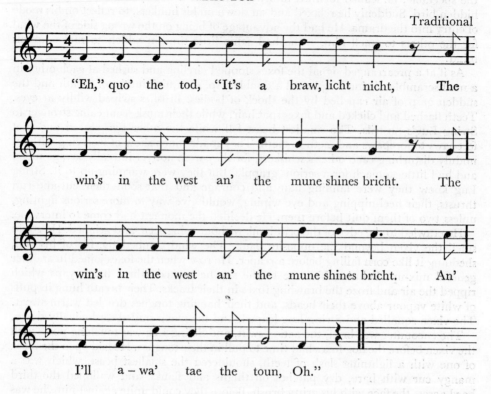

"Eh," quo' the tod, "It's a braw, licht nicht, The

win's in the west an' the mune shines bricht. The

win's in the west an' the mune shines bricht. An'

I'll a-wa' tae the toun, Oh."

'I was doon amang yon shepherd's scrogg
I'd like tae been worrit by his dogs
But, by my sooth, I minded his hogs
The nicht I cam' tae the toun O.'

He's ta'en the grey goose by the green sleeve,
'Eh, you auld witch! nae langer shall ye live;
Your flesh it is tender, your bones I maun prieve
For that I cam' tae the toun O.'

Up gat the auld wife oot o' her bed,
An' oot o' the window she shot her auld head:
'Eh, gudeman, the grey goose is dead,
An' the tod's been in the toun, O.'

P. 137 in *101 Scottish Songs* selected by Norman Buchan, Collins, 1962, £0·40.

140

*The Fox and the Salmon Fisher*

A fisher whilom lay
Beside a river for till get
His nets that he had there set.
A little ludge there had he made
And therewithin a bed he had
And eke a little fire alswa.
A door there wes, withouten ma.
Ae nicht his nets for till see,
He rase and there weel lang dwelt he.
And when that he has done his deed,
Toward his ludge again he gaed
And with licht of the little fire
That in the ludge was burnand schir
Intil the ludge a fox he saw
That fast gan on a salmon gnaw.
Then till the door he went in hy
And drew ane sword deliverly
And said, 'Traitor thou maun here out.'
The fox that wes in full great doubt
Lookit about some hole to see
But nane issue there couth he see
But where the man stood sturdily.
A lawn mantle then him by
Lyand upon the bed he saw,
And with his teeth he gan it draw
Atour the fire; and when the man
Saw his mantle lie burnand than
Till redd it ran he hastily.
The fox gat out than in great hy,
And held his way his warren till.
The man thocht him beguilit ill
That he his salmon swa had tynt
And also had his mantle brynt,
And the fox scatheless gat his way.

*Barbour: The Bruce*
*Bk. XIX, ll. 649–683*

Printed in Scotland by Her Majesty's Stationery Office at HMSO Press, Edinburgh
Dd 398226 K32 3/76 (13021)